REGIONAL TRAMWAYS

YORKSHIRE AND NORTH EAST OF ENGLAND

REGIONAL TRAMWAYS

YORKSHIRE AND NORTH EAST OF ENGLAND

PETER WALLER

PEN & SWORD
TRANSPORT

First published in Great Britain in 2016 by
Pen & Sword Transport
an imprint of
Pen & Sword Books Ltd
47 Church Street, Barnsley South Yorkshire S70 2AS

ISBN 978 1 47382 3 846

Pen & Sword Books Ltd incorporates the imprints of Pen & Sword Archaeology, Atlas,
Aviation, Battleground, Discovery, Family History, History, Maritime, Military, Naval,
Politics, Railways, Select, Social History, Transport, True Crime, and Claymore Press,
Frontline Books, Leo Cooper, Praetorian Press, Remember When, Seaforth Publishing and
Wharncliffe.

For a complete list of Pen & Sword titles please contact:
Pen & Sword Books Limited
47 Church Street, Barnsley, South Yorkshire, S70 2AS, England
E-mail: enquiries@pen-and-sword.co.uk
Website: www.pen-and-sword.co.uk

Printed and bound by Replika Press Pvt. Ltd.
Typset by Pen & Sword Books Ltd
A CIP record for this book is available from the British Library

CONTENTS

ABBREVIATIONS

BEC:	British Electric Car Co Ltd
BET:	British Electric Traction
BTC:	British Transport Commission
EMB:	Electro-Magnetic Brake Co
ER&TCW:	Electric Railway & Tramway Carriage Works Co
GNP:	Glasgow Numerical Printing Co
LMS:	London, Midland & Scottish Railway
LNER:	London & North Eastern Railway
LPTB	London Passenger Transport Board
LT:	London Transport
LUT:	London United Tramways
M&G:	Mountain & Gibson Ltd
M&T:	Maley & Taunton Ltd
MET:	Metropolitan Electric Tramways
PCC:	Presidents' Conference Car
UDC:	Urban District Council
UEC:	United Electric Car Co Ltd
VAMBAC:	variable automatic multi-notch braking and control

KEY TO MAPS

Passenger lines
Lines closed before 1 January 1945
Non-passenger lines
Lines of neighbouring operators – open at 1 January 1945
Lines of neighbouring operators – closed at 1 January 1945
Passenger lines built opened after 1 January 1945
Lines under construction at 1 January 1945 – never completed

PREFACE

This is the second in a series that is intended, ultimately, to cover all the tramways of the British Isles. Its focus is on those tramway systems in Yorkshire and north-east England that operated after 1945. However, it also provides an overview of tramway development from the horse-tram era onwards in the region. Following the introduction, individual chapters deal with each of the first-generation tramways that survived into 1945, with a map that shows the system as it existed at 1 January 1945 and a fleet list of all the trams operated after that date. The Yorkshire and north-east region also includes two second-generation tramways – Sheffield Supertram and Tyne & Wear Metro – which are covered.

The majority of illustrations in the book are drawn from the collection of the Online Transport Archive; in particular, I am grateful to Barry Cross, Bob Jones, Hamish Stevenson and John Meredith, as well as to the late Drew Crighton, Marcus Eavis, Jim Joyce, Harry Luff, Phil Tatt and Tony Wickens – all of whose negatives or collections are now in the care of OTA. Martin Jenkins has been a great help in tracking down certain images and providing information. I'd also like to thank Hugh McAulay, for providing information about the tramways of Newcastle and Gateshead, and Richard Wiseman for permission to reproduce his view of Rotherham. Every effort has been made to ensure complete accuracy. Unfortunately, the records available are not always consistent and, with the passage of time, the number of those with detailed knowledge is sadly declining. Likewise every effort has been made to ensure the correct attribution of photographs. It goes without saying that any errors of fact or attribution are the author's and any corrections should be forwarded to him care of the publishers.

Peter Waller,
Shrewsbury,
March 2015

INTRODUCTION

The tramway age in Yorkshire and north-east England predated the Tramways Act, as the first tramcars to operate in the region commenced in Darlington on 1 January 1862. This was one of the pioneering horse tramways opened in Britain by the American entrepreneur George Francis Train, following on from his first line that had opened in Birkenhead two years earlier. However, without a legal framework to operate the trams, Train was subject to various legal impediments, including being sued for the loss of a greyhound, and the line ceased operation on 1 January 1865 and was quickly dismantled. The operating company was wound up in December the same year.

The legal framework that Train lacked in Darlington came with the passing of the Tramways Act in 1870. The Act authorised local authorities to grant the rights to operate tramways within the local area to companies for a period of twenty-one years; construction of the tramway could either be undertaken by the authority and leased to the operator or by the operator itself. The Act also imposed a duty upon the operator of maintaining the strip of road 18in either side of the outer running rails. This was the Achilles' heel of the Act because roads were generally badly maintained – if they were maintained at all – and the

The first horse trams built for Sheffield Tramways Co were twelve, such as No 9 seen here, built by Starbuck Car & Wagon Co of Birkenhead for the Attercliffe route – the first section of the horse tramway to open (on 6 October 1873) and extended to Tinsley on 7 May 1874.
Barry Cross Collection/ Online Transport Archive

Hull Street
Tramways Co No 15 is pictured on the Beverley Road to Pier Head route in the mid-1890s, shortly before the company sold out to Hull Corporation.
Barry Cross Collection/ Online Transport Archive

creation of this well-managed strip in the middle meant that it was available to all road users and the tram became perceived as causing delays to other road users. At the end of the twenty-one-year lease, or periodically thereafter, the local authority was entitled to purchase the assets of the company at a written-

down value. This further weakness in the Act dissuaded the leaseholders from investing further in the business as the potential selling price would not reflect

No fewer than five horse trams are visible in this view of Newcastle & Gosforth Tramways & Carriage Co's terminus at Gosforth High Street. In 1893 the company had a fleet of 44 cars and 272 horses operating over a network of 17 route miles. Barry Cross Collection/Online Transport Archive

the investment undertaken. The 1870 Act was subsequently amended, most notably with the Light Railways Act of 1896, but represented the basis upon which most tramways were built.

There were, following the experiment in Darlington, a number of horse tram operators in the area covered by the volume. The earliest was in Leeds, where Leeds Tramways Co introduced a standard gauge service on 16 September 1871; following acquisition by Leeds Corporation on 2 February 1894, the last horse trams operated in the city on 13 October 1901. Horse trams, again standard gauge, ran in Sheffield under the aegis of Sheffield Tramways Co on 6 October 1873. The system eventually extended to five routes; company operation ceased on 11 July 1896 when Sheffield Corporation took over. The

A double-deck horse tram of Sunderland Tramways Co; the company introduced its first service in April 1879 with the operation passing to the corporation twenty years later. *Barry Cross Collection/ Online Transport Archive*

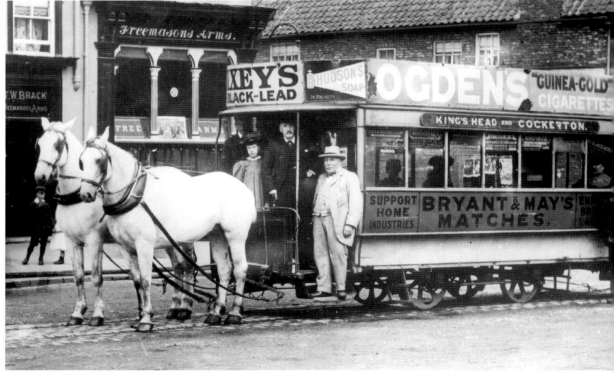

One of Stockton & Darlington Steam Tramway Co's 3ft 0in gauge horse trams stands in front of the Freemasons' Arms on Bondgate in Darlington. It is suggested that the elderly gentleman standing on the platform at the front dressed in white is from the company's then owners – Imperial Tramways. If that is the case, the image must date to between 1898, when Stockton & Darlington Steam Tramway Co was acquired by Imperial Tramways, and August 1903, when horse tram services ceased. *Barry Cross Collection/Online Transport Archive*

final horse cars operated on 30 May 1903. Sheffield was followed by Dewsbury, Batley & Birstal (sic) Tramways Co, again of standard gauge, on 25 July 1874; these lasted until replaced by steam trams six years later. Horse trams first operated in Hull on 9 January 1875. Originally operated by Continental & General Tramways Co, ownership passed to Hull Street Tramways Co in 1876. In total, some nine route miles of standard gauge track were operated; however, financial problems resulted in the company going into liquidation in 1889 and the Holderness Road route being sold to Drypool & Marfleet Steam Tramways Co. Ownership of the remaining part of the horse network passed to Hull Corporation in late 1896 for £12,500. The last horse trams operated on 30 September 1899. Under the auspices

of Newcastle & Gosforth Tramways & Carriage Co, horse trams were introduced to Newcastle-upon-Tyne on 5 December 1878. With the corporation desirous of taking over to electrify the system, company-operated standard gauge horse trams ceased operation on 13 April 1901 without replacement. The corporation then exercised powers of compulsory purchase and electrified the system. In Sunderland, the Sunderland Tramways Co introduced horse trams on 28 April 1879; following the takeover by the corporation on 31 December 1899 and the decision to electrify the network, the final standard gauge horse trams operated on 19 February 1901. Horse trams were reintroduced to the streets of Darlington on 10 October 1880 by Stockton & Darlington Steam Tramway Co; the company adopted the 3ft 0in

The City of York possessed a 4ft 0in gauge horse tramway that extended just over 3 route miles. Operated by York Tramways Co between 1880 and 1886, and by City of York Tramways Co Ltd between then and the corporation takeover, a total of nine double-deck and one single-deck trams were used; one of the former is illustrated here.
Barry Cross Collection/Online Transport Archive

Among the horse trams operated by South Shields Tramways & Carriage Co were six, Nos 11-16, that were supplied by Ashbury Railway Carriage & Wagon Co. Nicknamed 'Bedsteads', the open single-deck cars could accommodate eighteen seated passengers. Popular in fine weather (for obvious reasons) the sextet was limited to operating between Laygate Lane and the Pier Head. In later years the cars were fitted with a rudimentary top cover. Barry Cross Collection/Online Transport Archive

One of Keighley Tramway Co's horse trams is pictured at the Ingrow Bridge terminus of the first tram route to serve the town.
Barry Cross Collection/ Online Transport Archive

Steam trams were introduced by Dewsbury, Batley & Birstal Tramways Co on 10 April 1880. In all, eleven steam locomotives, all built by Merryweather, were operated over the 4¹/₄ route miles that the company leased. In 1880 one of the locomotives is pictured attached to ex-horse trailer No 9, one of five (Nos 6-10) built by Starbuck Car & Wagon Co between 1876 and 1880.
Barry Cross Collection/Online Transport Archive

gauge and the horse trams ran until 18 August 1903 when they were withdrawn to permit the track to be regauged to 3ft 6in and electrified. Horse trams of 4ft 0in gauge were introduced to the streets of York by York Tramways Co Ltd on 26 October 1880; operation was taken over by York Tramways Co Ltd on 1 January 1886, a subsidiary of Imperial Tramways, and the operation passed to corporation

ownership on 27 February 1909. Horse trams first operated in Bradford on 1 February 1882 when they were introduced by Bradford Tramways Co; following acquisition by Bradford Corporation, the last horse trams were withdrawn by early 1903. The first horse trams served South Shields under the ownership of South Shields Tramways Co on 1 August 1883. Financial problems, however, led to the

One of Sunderland Tramway Co's experimental steam trams – one of the three locomotives that the company owned – is pictured at Roker.
Barry Cross Collection/Online Transport Archive

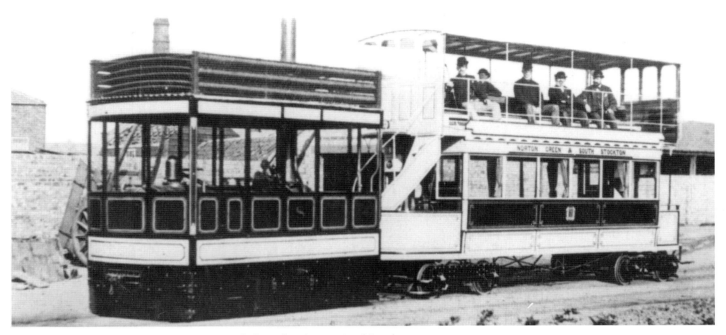

A Merryweather steam tram locomotive, believed to be No 8, of Stockton & Darlington Steam Tramways Co Ltd, at Stockton Depot. This was built in 1881 for North Staffordshire Tramways and acquired by Stockton & Darlington by 1884. The trailer is No 15, which was built in 1897, and was the only covered-top bogie trailer owned; the remainder were all open-top four-wheel cars. No 15 was built for the Norton Green to South Stockton (Thornaby) service in c1885. Barry Cross Collection/Online Transport Archive

Huddersfield Corporation became the first municipal operator of trams in Britain when, on 11 January 1883, it inaugurated its first service. One of the corporation's Kitson locomotives with double-deck trailer is seen at Lockwood in c1896. Barry Cross Collection/Online Transport Archive

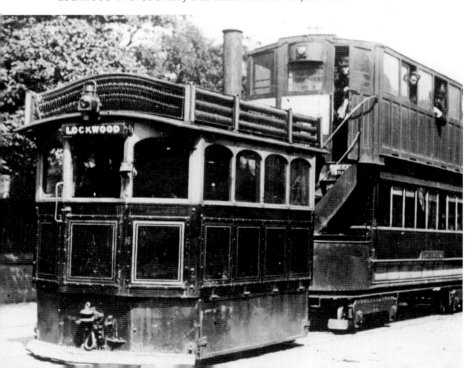

cessation of services on 30 April 1886. However, a new company, South Shields Tramways & Carriage Co, was set up to restart operation, commencing services on 28 March 1887. Horse trams survived in South Shields until 31 January 1906 when they were withdrawn to permit the electrification of the system under the auspices of the corporation. The last horse tramway to open in the region covered in this book was that which served Keighley. The first section was opened by Keighley Tramways Co Ltd on 8 May 1889. The route, built to the 4ft 0in gauge, ultimately ran for about $2\frac{1}{4}$ route miles linking Utley to Ingrow via the town centre. The operation, which was never financially successful, passed to Keighley Corporation on 21 September 1901, and the last horse trams operated on 21 September 1904.

Following experiments in 1876 and 1878, the first steam trams in the region were operated by Dewsbury, Batley & Birstal Tramways Co from 10 April 1880; these were, in fact, the first steam trams to operate on the public highway in England. The company was taken over by BET in 1902 and the local authorities

exercised their powers to also acquire the track. The lines were then reconstructed for use by electric trams. Leeds Tramway Co introduced steam trams on 17 June 1880; these were also taken over by the corporation on 2 February 1894 and last operated on 1 April 1902. In Sunderland

Huddersfield was unusual in that horse traction was adopted after the operator had already introduced steam trams. A total of four horse trams, Nos 7/8 and 12/13, were built for the corporation by Ashbury Railway Carriage & Iron Co Ltd of Manchester in 1885. Destined for a short life in Yorkshire, all four, including No 7 seen here, were sold to the Stockport & Hazel Grove Tramway Co Ltd in 1890/91 following the cessation of Huddersfield's horse tram operation on 1 April 1888.
Barry Cross Collection/Online Transport Archive

Bradford Tramways & Omnibus Carriage Co Ltd locomotive No 31 was one of twenty-four, Nos 12-35, supplied by Thomas Green & Sons Ltd of Leeds between 1888 and 1894. It is seen here attached to double-deck trailer No 23, which was delivered in 1885, although the manufacturer is unknown.
Barry Cross Collection/

Numerically, the highest locomotive in Bradford & Shelf Tramways Co Ltd, No 14 was one of seven acquired from Thomas Green & Sons Ltd between 1887 and 1893, five of which were replacements for earlier locomotives in the fleet.
Barry Cross Collection/ Online Transport Archive

the Tramways Co experimented with steam tram operation between 15 October 1880 and the middle of the following year, but disruption to other traffic and frequent breakdowns meant that they only survived seven months. Steam trams operated also experimentally in York in 1881, but horse traction was retained.

When acquiring its steam locomotives, Gateshead & District Tramways shopped locally, buying all sixteen of its steam locomotives from Black Hawthorn & Co. Fifteen received fleet numbers; the sixteenth was deemed too heavy and returned to its manufacturer. Engine No 13 is seen with one of the two larger trailers, either Nos 15 or 16, that were supplied by Lancaster Carriage & Wagon Co in 1889.
Barry Cross Collection/ Online Transport Archive

Steam engine No 2 and trailer of North Shields & District Tramways Ltd. The company operated over about 2$\frac{1}{2}$ miles of 3ft 0in gauge track between 1884 and 1897 when it was taken over by BET.
Barry Cross Collection/Online Transport Archive

Physically separate from Darlington horse trams, steam trams were introduced by Stockton & Darlington Steam Tramway Co on a 4ft 0in gauge route from Stockton to Norton – a distance of 3$\frac{1}{4}$ miles – on 17 November 1883. The route was extended and services eventually operated over 6$\frac{1}{4}$ route miles. The company was taken over by Stockton & District Tramways Co in 1893; this itself became a subsidiary of Imperial Tramways in 1896. Steam trams were withdrawn later the same year to permit the route's regauging (to 3ft 7in) and electrification. Steam trams first appeared on the streets of Huddersfield on 11 January 1883. The council had failed to find a company willing to take on the lease for operations, so the corporation itself took it on, thus becoming the first municipal operator of public transport in the British Isles. Huddersfield adopted the slightly unusual gauge of 4ft 7$\frac{3}{4}$in to enable conventional standard gauge railway wagons to operate over its metals. Huddersfield was also unusual in that horse trams were introduced to the town later than the steam trams;

horse trams operated from 9 May 1885 through to 1 April 1888, and the last steam trams operated on 21 June 1902. In neighbouring Bradford there were two operators of steam trams. The first to commence operation, on 3 August 1882, was Bradford Tramways & Omnibus Co, which already operated horse trams. In all, the company operated just over 17 route miles of 4ft 0in gauge track, and the last steam tram operated on 5 June 1902, shortly after Bradford Corporation took over the company's assets on 1 February 1902. The second operator was Bradford & Shelf Tramways Co, which operated over 7$\frac{1}{2}$ route miles (again of 4ft 0in gauge) with steam from 8 September 1884. Bradford Corporation took over on 31 January 1902 with the last steam trams operating on 1 April 1903. On the Durham Coast, steam trams were introduced to Hartlepool by Hartlepool Steam Tramways Co Ltd on 2 August 1884. A total of six steam locomotives operated on the 3ft 6in gauge route that linked Hartlepool with West Hartlepool. The company failed financially and

To open the Roundhay tramway in 1891, Stephenson Carriage & Wagon Co of New York supplied six twenty-two-seat single-deck cars, Nos 75-80 – the last of which is illustrated here. The fleet was subsequently augmented by the acquisition of three single-deck trailer cars. Following the takeover by Leeds Corporation, seven of the fleet were retained to operate as trailer cars. Barry Cross Collection/Online Transport Archive

services ceased on 21 February 1891. In the north-east, standard-gauge steam trams of Gateshead & District Tramways Co commenced operating on 22 October 1883. Eventually three routes, with a route mileage of 6¹/₄ miles, were operated. On 12 November 1897 the company was taken over by BET with a view to electrification and the last steam trams operated on 8 May 1901. The 3ft 0in-gauge horse trams of Tynemouth & District Tramways were taken over by North Shields & District Tramways Ltd in 1884 and steam trams were introduced; following purchase by BET in 1897, the steam trams were withdrawn in 1900, and the tramway regauged to 3ft 6in and electrified. Following its acquisition of the Holderness Road route from Hull

Street Tramways Co in 1889, Drypool & Marfleet Steam Tramways Co introduced steam trams on 22 May 1889. The company was acquired by the corporation for £15,000 in 1899 and the last steam tram operated on 13 January 1901.

The first electric trams to operate in the region were the standard gauge single-deck cars of the Roundhay company in Leeds on 11 November 1891; these were the first electric trams powered from the overhead to operate in Great Britain other than a short experimental installation in Edinburgh the previous year. Leeds Corporation commenced operating electric trams on 28 July 1897. Neighbouring Bradford also witnessed an early experiment in the use of overhead electric trams when, on 12 March 1892, the Halifax-born Michael Holroyd Smith – who earlier pioneered the electrification of the tramway at Blackpool – ran a short line between Cheapside and Manor Row; the demonstration lasted three weeks. The electric trams of Bradford Corporation

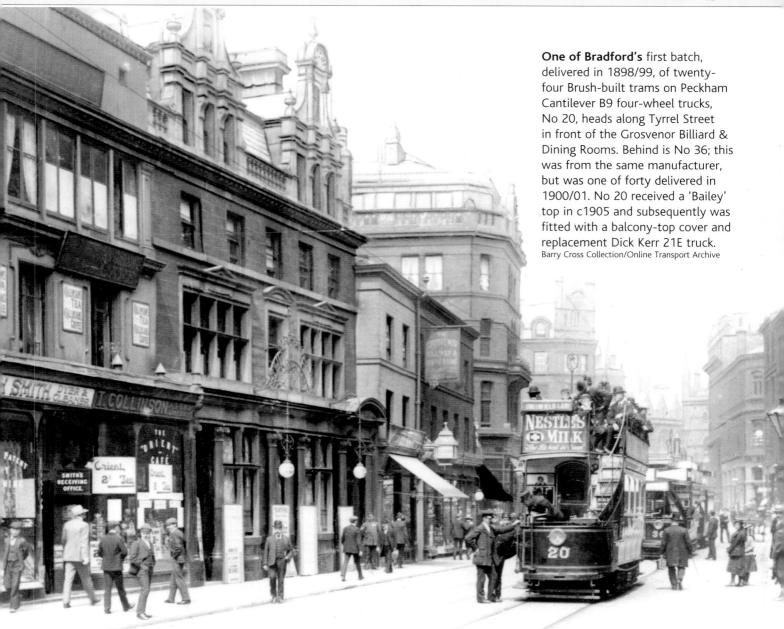

did not commence operation until 30 July 1898.

Bradford Corporation was beaten by the 3ft 6in gauge trams of Halifax Corporation, which commenced operation on 29 June 1898. Ultimately the system stretched for 39 route miles, connecting with Bradford's 4ft 0in trams at Queensbury, Shelf and Bailiff Bridge, and with Huddersfield's 4ft $7^3/_4$in system at Brighouse. Although experimenting briefly with trolleybuses, Halifax trams were ultimately replaced by buses, with the last conversion on 14 February 1939.

The first electric cars in Huddersfield commenced operation on 14 February 1902 with the system being just under 39 route miles at its maximum. Conversion to trolleybus began in 1933 following a change of manager and the last tram operated on 29 June 1940. Huddersfield was one of a handful of tramways to cease operation during the Second World War.

Bradford was not alone in selecting the 4ft 0in gauge; to the north and west of the city were the tramways of Mid-Yorkshire Tramways Co and Keighley Corporation.

Halifax Corporation No 62 stands in front of the impressive Town Hall in Sowerby Bridge, which was situated on the long route west to Mytholmroyd. No 62 was one of a batch of twenty-four open-top cars, Nos 59-82, delivered from Brush in 1903 that were fitted with Brush A cantilever trucks. No 62 was one of the cars fitted with an open-canopy top cover in 1912. Barry Cross Collection/Online Transport Archive

A number of Huddersfield trams stand outside the corporation's depot and workshop at Great Northern Street awaiting the scrapyard. On the left is No 80; this was one of a batch of ten cars, Nos 77-86, built by UEC on Preston 21E trucks that were new in 1913. On the right is No 40; this was one of five cars delivered in 1902 – the others being Nos 63-66 – that were the first top-covered cars delivered new to the corporation. Built by BEC it was fitted with a BEC SB60 four-wheel truck.
W. B. Stocks/Barry Cross Collection/Online Transport Archive

The former operated $3^1/_2$ miles of route leased from Shipley UDC, commencing operation on 23 July 1903. Linked to the Bradford network, operation passed to Bradford Corporation on 30 April 1904. Keighley Corporation, having taken over the horse trams of Keighley Tramways Co on 12 February 1901, commenced operation on 12 October 1904, with the last horse trams having operated on 21 September 1904. The system extended over nearly $3^1/_2$ miles and was replaced by trolleybuses, with the final tram running on 19 December 1924. Proposals to link the trams of Keighley with those of Bradford Corporation – a distance of only two miles – were never completed.

The remaining electric tramways within West Yorkshire were all standard gauge. Connecting with the 4ft 0in gauge trams of Bradford Corporation at Birkenshaw were the electric trams of Yorkshire (Woollen District) Electric Tramways Co Ltd, a subsidiary of BET, which commenced operation of its first section, from Dewsbury to Thornhill, on 18 February 1903. The system eventually totalled just under $22^3/_4$ route miles, and the fleet included trams owned by Batley Corporation but operated by the company. The company trams were replaced by bus between 19 March 1932 and 31 October 1934. A second company to serve Dewsbury, but physically separate from Yorkshire (Woollen District), was Dewsbury, Ossett & Soothill Nether Tramways. Although

Mid-Yorkshire Tramways Co operated trams for a relatively brief period before being acquired by Bradford Corporation. The company owned a fleet of ten cars, of which this is believed to be No 3, that were built by Hurst Nelson on Hurst Nelson S4W four-wheel trucks. All ten passed to Bradford Corporation, as Nos 230-39, where six were later rebuilt with open-balcony top covers. Barry Cross Collection/Online Transport Archive

One of Keighley Corporation's twelve double-deck trams stands on the railway bridge adjacent to the station in Keighley. This was one of the original batch of ten trams delivered in 1904; when delivered all ten were open-top, but open-balcony top covers were fitted to all between 1910 and 1912. Barry Cross Collection/Online Transport Archive

the track was owned by Dewsbury and Ossett corporations, operation was in the hands of National Electric Construction Co's subsidiary and commenced on the three mile long route on 13 November 1908. The company was acquired by BET in 1931 and the trams were replaced by Yorkshire (Woollen District) buses on 19 October 1933. Further to the east were the two sections of Yorkshire (West Riding) Electric Tramways Co Ltd. Wakefield & District Light Railway Co constructed $15\frac{1}{2}$ route miles of track linking Wakefield to Sandal, Agbrigg, Ossett and Leeds (where a connection with the corporation system was made at Thwaite Gate) along with a branch from Rothwell Haigh to Rothwell. The system opened on 15 August 1904. The following year it became a subsidiary of Yorkshire (West Riding) Electric Tramways Co Ltd and, on 1 June the same year, through running commenced to central Leeds. Leeds Corporation took over operation of the Rothwell branch at the same time. The system was converted to bus operation, with the last trams operating on 25 July 1932. Leeds Corporation operation over the route to Rothwell ceased, along with the Leeds-Wakefield service, on 31 May 1932; thereafter corporation trams served Hunslet for more than a quarter of a century. Separated from the routes around Wakefield was the $7\frac{3}{4}$ - mile line from Normanton via Castleford to Pontefract; also owned by Yorkshire (West Riding) Electric Tramways Co Ltd, this line opened on 29 October 1906, and the trams were replaced by buses on 1 November 1925.

Moving south, the first standard gauge electric trams served Sheffield on 5 September 1899, the corporation having taken over the horse trams of Sheffield Tramways Co on 11 July 1896. The last horse trams in the city operated on 11 November 1902. Rotherham Corporation commenced operation on 31 January 1903. Apart from the through route to

Two of Yorkshire (Woollen District) Electric Tramways Co's fleet pass on Market Street, Cleckheaton. On the right is No 39, one of forty-two open-top cars, Nos 7-48, that were supplied by Brush on Brush A four-wheel trucks in 1902/03. By the date of the photograph all the batch had been fitted with top covers.
Barry Cross Collection/Online Transport Archive

Sheffield via Templeborough, which was retained and upgraded in the 1930s with the introduction of eleven brand-new single-ended trams, the entire Rotherham system was converted to trolleybus or bus between 1929 and 1934. At Rotherham Bridge, where the system's depot was located, the corporation metals connected with those of Mexborough & Swinton Tramways Co. This company commenced operation on 6 February 1907. Initially its trams were powered by the Dolter surface-contact method rather than by conventional overhead; problems with the system led to its swift replacement and normal overhead was introduced. The last Dolter cars operated on 30 July 1908. From 1915 Mexborough & Swinton operated trolleybuses and the twenty-strong fleet of trams was replaced by trolleybuses during 1928 and 1929. The

Seen at the Dewsbury terminus of the Dewsbury, Ossett & Soothill Nether Tramway is one of the original batch of eight cars, Nos 1-8, delivered by Brush in 1908. Fitted with Brush 21E four-wheel trucks, all eight were eventually fitted with open-balcony top covers.
Barry Cross Collection/Online Transport Archive

The southernmost terminus of Yorkshire (West Riding) Electric Tramways Co Ltd was situated at Sandal, where, close to the cricket ground, No 42 is pictured. This was one of a batch of twenty-five cars, Nos 31-55, that was new in 1905. Built by UEC on Brill 21E four-wheel trucks, all twenty-five were delivered new with open-balcony top covers. Barry Cross Collection/Online Transport Archive

Sheffield No 123 was the last of a batch of twenty cars built by Brush on Brill 21E four-wheel trucks that were completed in 1900/01. A total of 172 similar cars, from a variety of builders, were supplied between 1899 and 1904; all were subsequently fitted with top-deck covers. Barry Cross Collection/ Online Transport Archive

Rotherham No 6 was one of a batch, Nos 1-12, that was built by ER&TCW on Brill 21E trucks in 1902 for the opening of the system. Barry Cross Collection/ Online Transport Archive

last company tram operated on 9 March 1929. A further link in the chain came with Dearne District Light Railways; this opened on 14 July 1924 – the last wholly new street tramway operator opened in Britain before the arrival of the second-generation tramways – and linked Mexborough and Swinton, at the Woodman Arms, south of Wath-upon-Dearne, with Barnsley and Thurnscoe. In an era of unrestricted bus operation, Dearne District was always going to struggle and the last of its fleet of thirty operated on 30 September 1933. Of its fleet, five were sold for further use in Falkirk, four to Lytham and equipment from the remainder to Hull. Although Dearne District served Barnsley, no physical connection was made to the standard-gauge tramways of Barnsley & District Electric Traction Co. This company commenced operation on 31 October 1902 and its fleet of fourteen cars survived until replacement by buses on 3 September 1930.

Separated from these operators was the final tramway to serve South Yorkshire – that of Doncaster Corporation. Although nominally standard gauge, the use of centre, rather than side, grooved rail resulted in an actual gauge of 4ft $7^5/_8$in. The corporation commenced operation on 2 June 1902 and the system, which ultimately operated forty-seven passenger cars, was converted to bus and trolleybus operation after 1928; the last route was converted on 8 June 1935. Doncaster was not alone in adopting the unusual centre-grooved track. Hull Corporation did likewise. Hull's electric trams first operated on 5 July 1899 and the system eventually extended over 21 route miles. In 1934 a co-ordination agreement was signed with East Yorkshire Motor Services, resulting in the outer section of corporation-operated routes passing to the company and the conversion of a number of tramway routes – such as beyond Dairycoates along the Hessle Road – to company-operated buses.

The Dearne District Light Railways was both the last new first-generation street electric tramway to open in Britain and also one of the shortest-lived. Operating between 1924 and 1933, the company possessed thirty single-deck cars, all of which were built by English Electric and fitted on Peckham P22 trucks. No 22 is seen at the terminus at Doncaster Road, Barnsley. Although the track of Barnsley & District Co is visible in the foreground, there was no physical connection between the two systems.
Barry Cross Collection/Online Transport Archive

The first corporation conversion to bus had already taken place – in 1931 – and, following a further tram to bus conversion in 1932, the remainder of the system was converted to trolleybus operation from 1937 onwards.

Farther up the Yorkshire coast, Scarborough Tramways Co operated a five-mile network of 3ft 6in gauge between 6 May 1904 and 30 September 1931 when, following the acquisition of the company by Scarborough Corporation, the trams were replaced by the buses of United Automobile Co. Another 3ft 6in gauge system was that which served York. The corporation took over the 4ft 0in horse trams of City of York Tramways Co Ltd on 27 February 1909 with the last horse trams operating on 7 September

1909. Under corporation ownership, the track was relaid to the narrower gauge and electric trams operated on 20 January 1910. The corporation's trams and trolleybuses were replaced in 1934/35 following a joint agreement between the corporation and West Yorkshire Road Car Co Ltd; the last trams operated on 16 November 1935.

The trams in York had been operated between 1886 and 1909 by a subsidiary of Imperial Tramways; a further subsidiary was involved with the operation of tramways along the south bank of the River Tees. Imperial Tramways Co acquired the horse trams of Middlesbrough & Stockton Co in 1878 and the steam trams of Stockton & District Co in 1896. Both operations were replaced by electric cars, operating on the unusual gauge of 3ft 7in, that commenced operation on 21 May 1898 under the name of Middlesbrough, Stockton & Thornaby Electric Tramways. The company operated the route, with its fleet of sixty passenger cars, until 2 April 1921 when operation passed to Middlesbrough

Corporation and to a joint committee of Stockton and Thornaby corporations. Middlesbrough continued to operate trams until 9 June 1934 when they were replaced by corporation-owned buses. Stockton became the sole operator of the joint section with Thornaby in 1930, with the final trams operated on 31 December 1931. The trams were again replaced by corporation-owned motorbuses.

Electric trams first appeared in Hartlepool on 19 May 1896 under the aegis of Hartlepool Electric Tramways, which was a subsidiary of General Electric Tramways Co Ltd. This company had purchased the disused lines of Hartlepool Steam Tramways Co Ltd in 1895 with a view to electrification. Operation of the 3ft 6in system passed to Hartlepool Electric Tramways Co Ltd

in 1899 and in 1912 to West Hartlepool Corporation, which operated the section in Hartlepool itself on a lease. The final trams operated on 25 March 1927, being replaced by trolleybuses owned by a joint committee of the two corporations. To the west lies Darlington; this had been home to one of the pioneering horse tramways operated by Train and a second horse system that was taken over by Imperial Tramways in 1896. The company planned to electrify the system, but Darlington Corporation exercised its powers and Corporation electric cars, operating on

Four open-top Doncaster trams are visible in this postcard, franked 28 September 1905, of the terminus in Station Road. Closest to the camera is No 3, one of the original batch of fifteen cars delivered in 1902 by ER&TCW that were fitted with Brill 21E four-wheel trucks. A number of the batch, but not No 3, were subsequently fitted with top covers.
Barry Cross Collection/ Online Transport Archive

A well-loaded Hull Corporation car heads along the Hessle Road route; the fact that the driver stands to one side of the platform allowing a non-uniformed man to take the tram's controls would suggest that this is a special event – also suggested by the interest being shown in the tram by the crowd along the road. Hull No 26 was one of five cars, Nos 26-30, that were built by Brill on Brill 21E four-wheel trucks.
Barry Cross Collection/ Online Transport Archive

the 3ft 6in gauge, commenced operation on 1 June 1904. In all, Darlington operated twenty-four passenger cars, including six acquired second-hand from Sheerness & District in 1918, with the last trams operating on 10 April 1926 with trolleybuses taking over.

Further to the north, on Wearside, there were two electric tramways. In 1900 Sunderland Corporation took over the operation of the standard gauge horse trams from Sunderland Tramways Co. The first electric cars operated, from Roker to Christ Church, on 15 August 1900, and the last horse trams operated the following year. Linked to the corporation tramway at its Grangetown terminus was the track of Sunderland District Electric Tramways Ltd. This company operated a largely single-track route with passing loops to Easington with branches to New Penshaw and Fencehouses – totalling $14\frac{1}{4}$ route miles. Operation commenced on 10 June 1905 but through running, Sunderland town centre did not start until 3 January 1921. The Sunderland District system was converted to buses owned by Sunderland District Omnibus Co with the last tram operating on 12 July 1925. Of the company's fleet of trams, eight were sold to Bolton and

In all, Scarborough Tramways Co operated twenty-nine trams; twenty-two were delivered new during 1904 and 1905 with the remaining seven being acquired second-hand from Ipswich. No 8, seen here, was one of a batch of fifteen, Nos 1-15, built by Brush and fitted with Brush AA four-wheel trucks. Seating capacity was forty-three. Barry Cross Collection/ Online Transport Archive

York Corporation was a relatively late arrival in terms of electric tram operation, with services not commencing until 20 January 1910. This view shows two of the original batch of cars, Nos 1 – suitably decorated for the opening – and 2. The system commenced operation with a batch of eighteen open-top cars built by Brush on Brush Radial four-wheel trucks.
Barry Cross Collection/ Online Transport Archive

The grandly titled Middlesbrough, Stockton & Thornaby Electric Tramways was a subsidiary of Imperial Tramways Co Ltd and operated, on the unusual gauge of 3ft 7in, until ownership passed to the local authorities in 1921. No 32 was one of a batch of fifty open-top cars built by Milnes in 1899 that were fitted with Peckham Cantilever maximum-traction bogies. In 1921, No 32 was one of the cars that passed to Stockton & Thornaby Joint Corporation Tramways. Barry Cross Collection/Online Transport Archive

sixteen to Grimsby Corporation for further use.

Along the south bank of the River Tyne there were three electric tramways. The first to open was in Gateshead, where the electric cars of Gateshead & District Tramways Co first operated on 8 May 1901, replacing the same company's steam trams. The Gateshead system was physically isolated until the 1920s, when on 12 January 1923 and in 1928, routes across the High Level and Tyne bridges respectively were opened, thus linking the Gateshead system to its larger neighbour's system; thereafter the history of the trams in Gateshead and Newcastle were inextricably linked. To the east, corporation-owned electric trams first operated in South Shields on 30 March 1906, having replaced the BET-owned horse trams. The last horse tram operated on 31 January 1906. Linked to South Shields, the single route operated

Middlesbrough No 134 is seen on Linthorpe Road on a postcard franked 3 September 1930. No 134 was one of the batch of nine open-balcony cars, Nos 132-40, acquired new by Middlesbrough Corporation in 1924 that were the only additions made by the corporation following its takeover of its part of the Imperial Tramways Co Ltd system in 1921. The cars were built by Hurst Nelson and fitted with Hurst Nelson 22E bogies.
Barry Cross Collection/Online Transport Archive

Following the division of Imperial Tramways' fleet between Middlesbrough Corporation and Stockton & Thornaby Joint Corporation Tramways in April 1921, the latter acquired thirty-one of the fifty Milnes-built bogie cars supplied for the system's opening in May 1898 (split twenty-two to Stockton and nine to Thornaby). One of the thirty-one, No 8, is seen here in the late 1920s; this was one of the cars owned by Thornaby Corporation.
Barry Cross Collection/Online Transport Archive

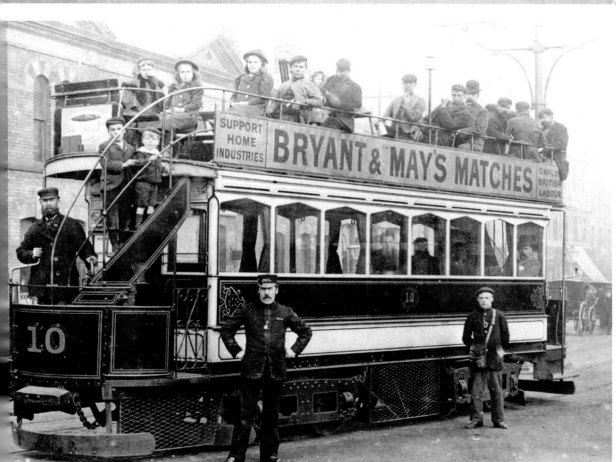

Electric trams were first introduced to Hartlepool and West Hartlepool by Hartlepool Electric Tramways. No 10, seen here in 1898, the year after it was built, was constructed by Milnes on Milnes-built bogies. Seating sixty-two, its original bogies were replaced in 1914.
Barry Cross Collection/ Online Transport Archive

Two of Sunderland's first batch of twelve cars, Nos 1 and 2, pass on the north side of the bridge across the River Wear. This initial batch was built by ER&TCW in 1900 on Brill 21E trucks. All twelve received balcony-top covers between 1904 and 1916, and lower-deck windscreens in 1914.
Barry Cross Collection/Online Transport Archive

Darlington Corporation Light Railways commenced operation in 1903 with sixteen single-deck combination cars, Nos 1-16, supplied by Milnes on McGuire four-wheel trucks. The cars seated twenty-six, with a fully enclosed central section and two open-end sections immediately behind each platform.
Barry Cross Collection/Online Transport Archive

by Jarrow & District Electric Traction Co Ltd, another BET subsidiary, commenced operation on 29 November 1906. The 2½-mile route linked Jarrow with the corporation terminus at Tyne Dock. There was joint running of the route; the last Jarrow & District tram ran on 30 June

1929, with buses providing a replacement service. Two of the ex-Jarrow cars were sold for further use by South Shields Corporation following the closure.

North of the River Tyne, the largest

Two Sunderland & District cars are pictured at Houghton-le-Spring. On the left is No 31; this was originally No 8, one of a batch of ten open-top cars built by ER&TCW on Brill 21E trucks in 1900, that was renumbered in 1905 following repair after it had overturned. On the right is No 28; this was one of a batch of fifteen cars, Nos 16-30, that were built with short-top covers by the French manufacturer Arbel/Blanc Misseron, that were fitted with the same manufacturer's version of the 21E four-wheel truck. This batch was relatively short-lived, being replaced by fifteen Brush-built cars in 1913. *Barry Cross Collection/Online Transport Archive*

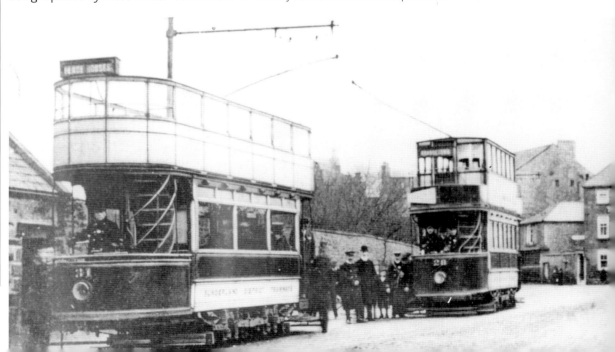

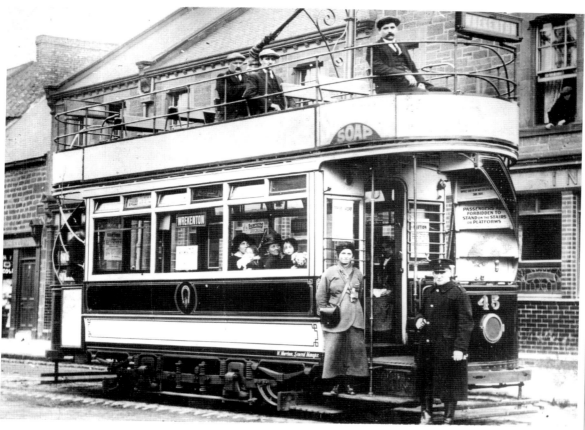

Gateshead & District No 45 was the last of a batch of twenty-five cars delivered by ER&TCW on Brill 21E trucks in 1901. Although the majority of the batch were rebuilt with balcony-top covers during 1924 and 1925, No 45 was rebuilt as a thirty-two-seat single-decker in c1920 and renumbered 51 about five years later. Barry Cross Collection/ Online Transport Archive

of the area's electric tramways was that serving Newcastle-upon-Tyne. In 1899, following the expiry of the twenty-one-year lease under which Newcastle & Gosforth Tramways & Carriage Co had operated the standard gauge horse trams, Newcastle Corporation assumed operation. The last horse trams operated on 13 April 1901 with electric services commencing on 16 December 1901. By 1928, a fleet of 300 cars operated over a route network of 51 miles. However, in

1935, the first trolleybuses were introduced and the decision was taken to convert the system to trolleybus and bus. To the east of the corporation system were the metals of Tyneside Tramways &

Jarrow & District Electric Tramways Co Ltd operated only twelve passenger cars in all during its twenty-three-year life; of these, No 9 illustrated here had perhaps the most interesting career. Built by Brush in 1902 on a Brush AA four-wheel truck, the tram was used by the company as an exhibition car, being displayed to potential customers in London until 1905. It was acquired by Jarrow & District in 1907. It is seen here after having been modified for service in Jarrow with six, rather than three, windows and modified stairs. Barry Cross Collection/ Online Transport Archive

One of South Shields' first batch of ten cars of 1905, Nos 1-10, No 9, is pictured in front of the Wouldhave Memorial. The ten cars were built by Hurst Nelson and fitted with Hurst Nelson 21E four-wheel trucks. Three of the type, but not No 9, were later fitted with top covers. The Wouldhave Memorial commemorated William Wouldhave (1751-1821), who was a pioneer in the development of lifeboats. Author's Collection

Tramroads Co. The company's standard gauge system extended from the West Gates at Gosforth Park, via Gosforth, where a connection was made with the corporation system at Henry Street and Wallsend, to North Shields. In Wallsend, there were connections to two corporation routes, thus permitting through running between Newcastle and North Shields. The company cars commenced operation on 22 September 1902. Powers to operate buses were obtained in 1920 and, on 6 April 1930, tram operation over the 11-mile long system ceased. At closure, the section between Gosforth and West Gates was acquired by Newcastle Corporation and survived until 1948. Of the company's fleet of thirty passenger cars, two were sold for further use by South Shields Corporation following closure. In North Shields, the trams of Tyneside Tramways & Tramroads Co met the 3ft 6in gauge trams of Tynemouth & District Electric Traction Co. The company, a subsidiary of BET, commenced operation of electric trams on 1 March 1901, following the withdrawal of the company's steam trams the previous year. The tramway, which was 4¼ miles

A view of Grainger Street in Newcastle taken during the interwar years with one of the 111-30 batch of cars heading away from the camera. The scene on the right is dominated by the Grainger Picture House; this was converted from a drapery store and opened originally on 1 December 1913. It reopened as the Grainger News Theatre on 2 December 1937. Barry Cross Collection/ Online Transport Archive

in length, survived until replaced by buses on 4 August 1931. The last cars to enter service, in 1927, were acquired from the Burton & Ashby line following the closure of the ex-Midland Railway-owned tramway by the LMS that year.

Tyneside Tramways & Tramroads Co No 16 descends Church Bank at Wallsend heading east towards Tynemouth. No 16 was one of seven open-top cars, Nos 12-18, built by ER&TCW in 1901 and fitted with Brill 21E four-wheel trucks.
Barry Cross Collection/Online Transport Archive

The only 3ft 6in gauge tramway on Tyneside was operated by Tynemouth & District Electric Traction Co Ltd between 1901 and 1931. No 12 was one of seven cars, Nos 12-18, built by ER&TCW on Brill 21E four-wheel trucks that were delivered in 1901.
Barry Cross Collection/ Online Transport Archive

BRADFORD

From the late 1920s, the tramcar had been on the retreat in Bradford largely in favour of the trolleybus. If the Second World War had not occurred, the system would have disappeared by the early 1940s. During 1939 the long route to Crossflatts was converted to trolleybus operation, but some 115 4ft gauge tramcars remained operational and, with the onset of hostilities in September 1939, trams were reintroduced to the Undercliffe route – a short working of the longer Greengates route converted to bus operation between Forster Square and Undercliffe on 7 April 1935 – on 11 September 1939. Also reopened on 11 September 1939 was a 680yd section – to Horsfall Playing Fields – of the former route to Shelf from Odsal, which had been converted to bus operation on 18 February 1935.

Although the two extensions were

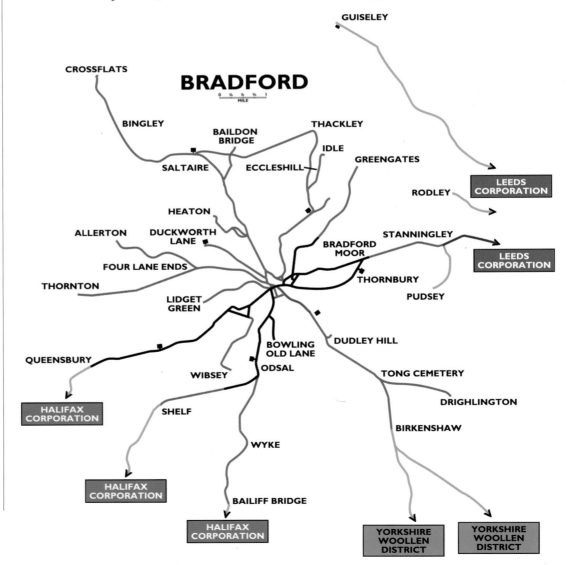

Map of the Bradford network as at 1945.

significant, they could not disguise the fact that the Bradford system was in poor physical condition, and lack of maintenance during the war exacerbated the problem. As a result, the corporation abandoned certain sections during the war: Thornbury-Stanningley on 19 October 1942, and the section from Odsal to Wyke and Bailiff Bridge on 11 June 1944. However, an application to convert the Wibsey route in 1942 was turned down by the Ministry of War Transport.

As a result, Bradford entered 1945 with a fleet of ninety-five trams operating over seven routes. One of these, however, was soon converted to bus operation, with the abandonment of the route to Wibsey on 7/8 January 1945. The last car to operate

Seen towards the end of the service's life, Bradford No 240 loads with passengers at the shelter on Hall Ings (nicknamed 'Tut's Tomb') with a service to Thornbury on route 9. On the right is a bus of Leeds Corporation, a reminder that – despite the difference in gauge – a through service operated between Leeds and Bradford via Stanningley between January 1907 and March 1918. Bradford No 240 wears the pale blue livery adopted during the war; there were, however, cars that retained the traditional dark blue livery until final withdrawal. F. E. J. Ward/Online Transport Archive (FEJW68)

over the route was No 253. The Wibsey conversion allowed for the disposal for scrap of a number of cars during the year: Nos 8, 45, 95, 119, 220/24/31/36/38/45/56/58. These included the final four of the 'Preston' cars and all were in the old livery.

Not all was negative, however, as trackwork was undertaken on the surviving routes. During 1945 the track

Bradford introduced the Ultimate form of ticketing in 1948; this is an example of the second style of these tickets, manufactured by Auto-Tickets from 1949.
Author's Collection

was relaid at the Bradford Moor terminus and at Horton Bank Top, as well as at the junction of Leeds Road and Well Street with preparation in hand for work on the junction of Leeds Road and Hall Ings. In early 1946 the track in Dirkhill Road and All Saints Road was replaced, resulting in the temporary rerouting of Queensbury trams via Park Avenue and Laisteridge Road. The work between Hall Ings and Well Street, on the Thornbury route, proved to be

the last major trackwork undertaken on the system and, with the reduction in its workload, the railgrinder was converted into an additional snowplough. Less promising, however, was the construction of a new siding into the engineer's yard at Bowling depot for the storage of withdrawn trams. To access the siding, cars needed their top decks removing to pass under a low railway bridge. The first tram to make the journey, on a lowloader, was No 129 in June 1949. Also, with improved frequencies on the bus service to Shelf, the service to Horsfall Playing Fields was reduced to evening peaks, evenings and Sunday mornings.

The tramway abandonment programme recommenced on 13 December 1947 with the conversion of the Bowling Old Lane route to bus operation; the last tram to operate over the route was No

On 22 August 1949, Bradford No 142 is pictured at the Queensbury terminus. This was the highest tram terminus in Britain and was one of three points where Bradford's trams made a connection with the 3ft 6in gauge trams of Halifax Corporation. By this stage the tram service to Queensbury was coming towards the end of its life; it was converted to bus operation three months later.
John Meredith/Online Transport Archive (81/10)

88. The next route to succumb was that to Undercliffe, which was converted to bus operation on 17 July 1948. The last tram on this route was No 93. Originally the route was to have been converted to trolleybus operation – indeed columns and new trolleybuses were purchased for such a conversion – but this did not happen and the equipment acquired was used elsewhere.

The reduction of the tramcar fleet resulting from these conversions saw the remaining trams reallocated at Thornbury to the western part of the depot using track disused since the 1930s and requiring a new connection with the track on Leeds Road; the terminus of the Thornbury route was also relocated at the same time by some 50yd. An indication that the life of the tramway system was drawing to a close came in February 1949 when No 86 entered Thornbury Works for an overhaul; it was released back into traffic in April 1949. The same month saw the final cars repainted at Thornbury.

Another change to the tramway fleet, consequent upon the acquisition of new AEC Regent IIIs, was that all trams numbered below 50 were renumbered by the addition of 100 to their original number at the end of March 1949; the cars affected were Nos 17/19, 20/23/26-29, 34/35/37 and 40/42-45/48 and 49. As No 130 was still extant, No 30 was not renumbered and, as the AEC Regent III destined for the same number was delayed, tram No 30 was withdrawn before renumbering was required.

The next conversion occurred on 23 July 1949 when the Bradford Moor route was converted to bus operation temporarily. Planning for the conversion had commenced two years earlier and trolleybuses were introduced to the route on 4 December 1949, thus recreating the cross-city Bradford Moor-Crossflatts service that had existed until the conversion of the Crossflatts service to trolleybus operation on 7 May 1939. The last car over the Bradford Moor route

Bradford No 250 stands on Leeds Road in front of Thornbury Depot; the route from Thornbury to the city centre was converted to bus operation on 4 March 1950. Two years later the buses were themselves replaced by trolleybuses. F. E. J. Ward/Online Transport Archive (FEJW69)

Pictured at Odsal on 22 August 1949, Bradford No 117 was one of the surviving trams to be renumbered following the acquisition of a batch of new AEC Regent III diesel buses. Until 1940, trolleybuses operated through Odsal and beyond to Oakenshaw; evidence of this can still be seen nine years later in the ex-trolleybus overhead.
John Meredith/Online Transport Archive (81/12)

was No 248. Less than four months later, on 5 November 1949, the route with the highest terminus in Britain – Queensbury via Horton Bank Top – was converted to bus operation. The last car was No 149, although its final journey was delayed by a broken span wire at Horton Bank Top.

The new year dawned with only two routes operational and thirty cars still in service. The next route converted, that to Thornbury, succumbed on 4 March 1950, although the track to Thornbury depot was retained until final closure to permit trams to access the works for minor repair. The last service car on the Thornbury route was No 229 and the same month saw the withdrawal of the last car, No 127, in the old dark blue

Pictured in Bankfoot Depot is Bradford No 104 suitably bedecked for its role as the corporation's official last tram on 6 May 1950. Following its ceremonial duties, the body of No 104 was transferred to Odsal, home of Bradford Northern RLFC, where it was used by the scorers until rescued for preservation later in the decade.
F. E. J. Ward/Online Transport Archive (FEJW297)

livery. The final day of the Bradford system was 6 May 1950. During the evening, trams provided a service to the speedway at Odsal – this required twenty-one of the surviving twenty-eight cars in the fleet – but this ceased at about 9.00 pm; this was the last use of the reserved track to Horsfall Playing Fields, with No 109 being the last car to use it. The final service car, No 149, departed to Bankfoot from the city centre just after 11.00 pm; thereafter three cars – Nos 51, 104 (with the special party) and 140 – ran over the route to Bankfoot where there was a brief ceremony to mark the end of fifty-two years of electric tram operation.

With the demise of Bradford, the last 4ft 0in-gauge electric tramway in the UK had disappeared. It was not quite the end of the story, however, as No 104 – sold after closure to Odsal and reacquired for preservation and restoration in 1953 – ran over track at Thornbury Works between 1958 and 1966.

Bradford Depots

By 1945, the decline in the city's tramway network had resulted in a number of depots – such as Duckworth Lane and Saltaire – being closed to trams. There were, however, three depots that remained operational: Horton Bank Top, situated on the Queensbury route, which closed on 5 November 1949; Bankfoot, on Manchester Road, which closed on 6 May 1950 and was subsequently used for the scrapping of the redundant trams; and Thornbury, where the corporation's main workshops were also situated, which also closed on 6 May 1950. In addition, the depot at Bowling, closed as an operating depot for trams in 1938, was used both as a store for trams withdrawn after the war before their scrapping in the Permanent Way Yard adjacent to the depot. Thornbury Works was used, after 1950, for the storage of preserved trams, including ex-Sunderland No 100

and, following its restoration, Bradford No 104. For a brief period between 1958 and 1966, No 104 operated on track at Thornbury, drawing power from the trolleybus overhead. No 104 remained at Thornbury until the mid-1970s when it was transferred to the Bradford Industrial Museum at Moorside Mills.

Bradford Closures

8 January 1945
1 – Little Horton/Wibsey-City

13 December 1947
11 – Bowling Old Lane-City

18 July 1948
20 – Undercliffe-City

23 July 1949
30 – Bradford Moor-City

5 November 1949
3/2 – Queensbury/Horton Bank Top-City

4 March 1950
9 – Thornbury-City

6 May 1950
15 – Horsfall Playing Fields-Odsal-City

Bradford Fleet

17/19, 20/23/24/26-30, 31/34/35/37, 40/42-45/47-53/55-57, 61, 77/79, 81/83/86/88/89, 93-95/97/99, 102-105/08/09/11/30/78/81/89/95/96, 213/18/221-223/25-31/33/35/40/41/44/45/47-50/52-55

Starting with No 63 in September 1919 and concluding with No 14 in June 1931, a total of eighty-one open-canopy four-wheel cars were built in Thornbury Works, although there were minor variations in the height and width of the bodywork. All were fitted with Dick Kerr 21E trucks originally with the exception of eight fitted with Boving 21E trucks (originally Nos 23, 54/55, 60/63, 87, 125 and 205) and ten with Hurst Nelson trucks (originally Nos 14, 21/24, 33, 41, 54, 70, 81/82/86). Between October 1935 and May 1939 a number of the cars were fitted with Dick Kerr 21E trucks removed

The vast majority of Bradford trams that survived into 1945 were the eighty replacement cars, such as No 195, constructed at Thornbury Works between 1919 and 1931. By the date the last of these were built, the decision had already been made to convert the system largely to trolleybus operation. Barry Cross Collection/Online Transport Archive

from 'Preston' cars and were renumbered; the cars affected were as follows with the new fleet numbers in brackets: Nos 2 (213), 3 (218), 4 (226), 5 (230), 6 (231), 7 (233), 8 (240), 11 (247; this car had originally been numbered 70 on delivery); 12 (244), 13 (245), 14 (227), 15 (253), 16 (254), 21 (248), 33 (252), 39 (228; this car had originally been number 74 when new), 41 (250), 54 (255), 58 (241), 60 (249), 82 (229), 87 (235) and 125 (221). All the class were in service at the start of the war and eighty remained as at 1 January 1945. The only exception was the original No 119, which had been withdrawn in June 1944. In March 1949 a number of further

cars – Nos 17/19, 23/27/29, 34/35/37, 40/42-45/48/49 – were renumbered 117 and so on to vacate the number sequence to accommodate new AEC Regent IIIs then on order. Withdrawal of the type began again in August 1945, although the majority remained in service until 1949 and 1950, with the last cars taken out of service in May 1950 when the system closed. No 104 was the official last car; following a brief period in use at Bradford Northern's ground, Odsal, the car was subsequently restored and is now displayed at the Bradford Industrial Museum.

69, 70-75, 80, 90/92

Between September 1919 and September 1928, fifteen lowheight four-wheel cars – known as the 'Greengates' class – were built at Thornbury Works with bodies built by the corporation fitted to 21E trucks supplied by Boving (Nos 64-69) and Dick Kerr (Nos 70-75, 80, 90/92). In December 1936 No 69 received the Dick Kerr truck from 'Preston' car No 222 and was renumbered to 222. Nos 64-68 were withdrawn before the Second World War and withdrawal of the remainder of the type started in April 1948 with No 71. With the exception of No 69, withdrawn in May 1948, the remaining cars were withdrawn between June 1949 and May 1950.

107, 239

These two cars were the survivors of a batch of ten cars – the 'High Four Window' cars – built between 1917 and 1921 with bodies built at Thornbury Works. Four (Nos 129/60/79, 205) were originally fitted with Hurst Nelson 21E trucks; four (Nos 118/64, 214/18) with Boving 21E trucks; and the remaining two (Nos 158/63) with Dick Kerr 21Es. Three of the cars – No 118, which had already been renumbered 107, and Nos 158/64 – were retrucked with Dick Kerr 21E trucks

Ten of Bradford Corporation's 'Greengates' class of low height four-wheel cars survived into the post-war years. No 75 was originally new in September 1924 and remained in service until June 1949.
F. N. T. Lloyd-Jones/Online Transport Archive

Bradford No 107 was one of two survivors of a batch of ten cars built between 1917 and 1921. It is seen emerging from Horton Bank Top Depot towards the end of its life; No 107, originally numbered 118, remained in service until November 1949 when it was withdrawn following the conversion of the Queensbury and Great Horton routes to bus operation.
F. N. T. Lloyd-Jones/Online Transport Archive

from the 'Preston' cars in December 1936, and the latter two renumbered 239 and 232, respectively, at the same time. Apart from these three cars, the remaining seven trams were withdrawn by May 1939. Of the three survivors, No 232 was withdrawn in December 1944, leaving Nos 107 and 239 to be withdrawn in November 1949 and May 1948 respectively.

236/38/56/58

The last Bradford trams supplied by an outside contractor were forty-six cars supplied by English Electric between October 1919 and August 1921. Nos 213-58 were fitted with Dick Kerr 21E trucks, resulting in the type becoming

known as the 'Preston' cars. The bulk of the class was withdrawn before the Second World War, but ten – Nos 214-17/19/37/42/43/51/57 – were sold to Sheffield in 1942. The four surviving cars were withdrawn from service in Bradford during August and September 1945.

Works cars

Bradford Corporation employed a small fleet of dedicated works cars, the majority of which were converted from redundant passenger cars and used as snowploughs. One of the snowploughs (No S7) was withdrawn in January 1945 and one (No S1) in December 1947. The remainder were withdrawn either in June 1949 – Nos S2/3/10/11 – or May 1950 – Nos S4/6.

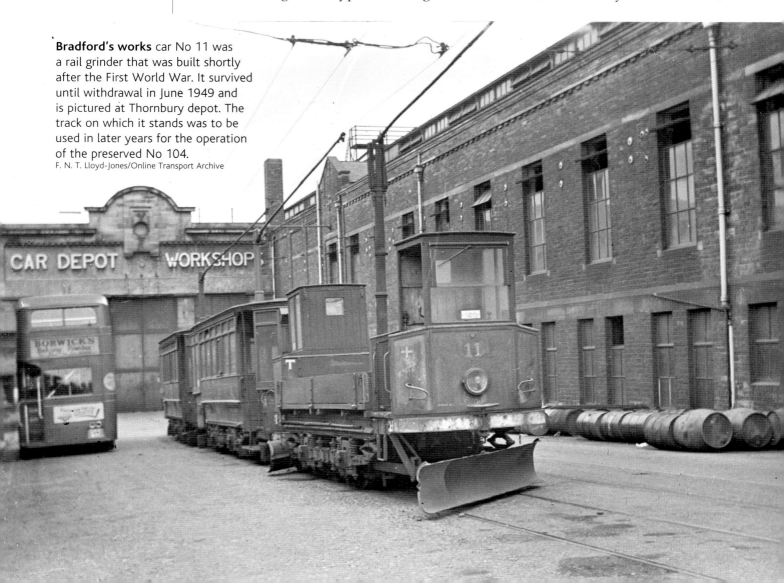

Bradford's works car No 11 was a rail grinder that was built shortly after the First World War. It survived until withdrawal in June 1949 and is pictured at Thornbury depot. The track on which it stands was to be used in later years for the operation of the preserved No 104.
F. N. T. Lloyd-Jones/Online Transport Archive

GATESHEAD

By 1945 Gateshead & District Tramways Co was one of a relatively small number of company-owned tramways that remained operational; many had either been taken over by local authorities on the expiry of their lease or had been converted to bus or trolleybus operation before the outbreak of the Second World War. Owned by BET, Gateshead & District was the last of this company's once significant tramway operations to survive.

The history of the trams in Gateshead was inextricably linked to those of Newcastle; if the systems had not been linked, Gateshead would likely have been converted before the war, but Newcastle's policy of conversion to trolleybus only became effective in the mid-1930s and, in the immediate post-war years, Gateshead's reluctance to convert to trolleybus effectively lengthened the life of trams on the north bank of the Tyne. The position of Gateshead & District was further complicated by the fact that

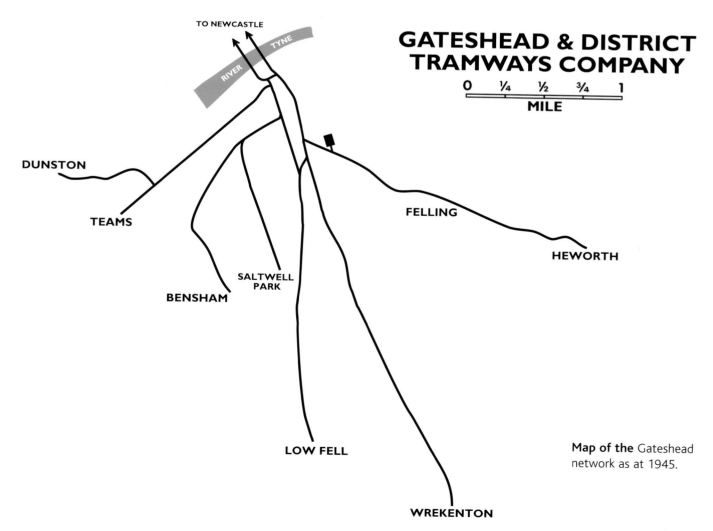

GATESHEAD & DISTRICT TRAMWAYS COMPANY

0   ¼   ½   ¾   1
MILE

TO NEWCASTLE

RIVER TYNE

DUNSTON

TEAMS

BENSHAM

SALTWELL PARK

FELLING

HEWORTH

LOW FELL

WREKENTON

Map of the Gateshead network as at 1945.

It was the tramway connections across the River Tyne constructed across the High Level and Tyne bridges, opened in 1923 and 1928 respectively, that ensured that thereafter the history of Gateshead & District's trams would be inextricably linked with those of Newcastle Corporation. Here Gateshead & District No 74 approaches the High Level Bridge from the south as it passes Gateshead station.
R. W. A. Jones/Online Transport Archive (GD8)

its assets could pass, at the expiry of its lease, to the local authorities through which it operated and, after the election of 1945 resulted in a Labour Government with a significant majority, the threat of the nationalisation of BET's transport interests.

Powers to operate trolleybuses in Gateshead existed – obtained in an Act passed in 1938 and extended in 1947 for a further three years – and during the war Newcastle had sought powers to operate trolleybuses over the bridges and into Gateshead. These proposals were, however, opposed by the Gateshead company as there would have been operational issues. That trolleybuses were still considered a potential means of transport in Gateshead post-war is

demonstrated by the company reportedly being potentially willing to invest in a replacement fleet of eighty-three trolleybuses at a cost of £600-700,000 over a two-year period; it was subsequently reported that the planned conversion was delayed by at least two years. In reality, however, uncertainty over the future ownership and the threat of nationalisation meant that the powers to operate trolleybuses were allowed to expire and when, in July 1950, a new Act was obtained, it explicitly stated that conversion would be to bus and that the company's name would be changed to Gateshead & District Omnibus Co. Originally the bill had been opposed by Gateshead Corporation, but an agreement in early 1950 resulted in the corporation's opposition being withdrawn. Two years earlier, in 1948, BET had offered the tramway operation to Gateshead Corporation and Felling Urban District Council – the two local authorities that had control – but this offer had been declined.

Although the future ownership and operation of the system remained uncertain, the tramway continued to function; indeed, there was investment in both track replacement and second-hand cars to supplement the fleet. In 1947, six fully enclosed double-deckers were acquired from Oldham and, the following year, five single-deckers were acquired from Newcastle. These cars were the last trams acquired by Gateshead & District. In terms of the infrastructure, trams were restored to the original Heworth terminus in 1944; the route had been cut back slightly in 1940 due to the war. During 1947 and 1948, using track and equipment bought second-

hand from Oldham, Salford and other operators, the Saltwell Park route was relaid as were the single-track sections of the routes to Wrekenton and Bensham; agreement was also reached with the LNER for the reconstruction of the West Street Bridge on the route to Dunston. This work, undertaken in June 1948 at a cost of £15,000, saw the clearance increased to 16ft 6in. Although this was still not sufficient to permit the operation of double-deck trams, it did allow for the unrestricted use of single-deck cars and double-deck buses over the route; previously, only cars with reduced-length trolleypoles could operate under the bridge.

The first Gateshead abandonment

Following Newcastle Corporation's conversion of the Gosforth Park section, all Gateshead & District trams serving Newcastle terminated at Newcastle Central station. Three Gateshead cars, with 1923-built No 64 closest to the camera, are seen at Central station before heading south across the Tyne. R. W. A. Jones/Online Transport Archive (GD7)

On 26 February 1950, Gateshead No 68 stands at Wrekenton. This service was converted to bus operation less than a fortnight later.
Tony Wickens/Online Transport Archive (268)

occurred on 16 April 1948 when the service linking Low Fell with Gosforth Park was withdrawn due to the conversion of the Gosforth Park section north of the Tyne to trolleybus operation; thereafter Gateshead's trams from Low Fell terminated at Newcastle Central station and through travellers had to change. However, once powers to operate buses and Gateshead Corporation's agreement had been gained, the company agreed a two-year schedule for complete conversion. The first routes to succumb were those to Wrekenton and Heworth,

Gateshead & District No 52 stands at Sheriff Hill on 26 February 1950; although the route through Sheriff Hill was converted to bus operation in March 1950, peak-hour services to Sheriff Hill continued for some months thereafter.
Tony Wickens/Online Transport Archive (264)

which were converted to bus operation on 4 March 1950. The new Gateshead buses to operate the routes had been delivered the previous month. The last Gateshead tram from Monument in Newcastle is uncertain, but is generally accepted as No 34. The last Newcastle tram from Gateshead – indeed the last Newcastle tram in service – was No 289. Although officially now bus operated, both routes retained some limited services – in peak hours to Heworth and Sheriff Hill and, latterly, on Sunday mornings alone to Wrekenton – through the summer. The exact date that these services ceased is unknown, but the removal of the overhead in September marked the final demise of these routes. Following this conversion, eighteen double-deck balcony cars were withdrawn for scrap.

The next routes withdrawn were those to Saltwell Park and Bensham, replaced by a circular bus route on 3 March 1951. Following this conversion, all the remaining double-deck trams were withdrawn and four single-deck cars – Nos 5, 9, 18 and 57 – were sold to British Railways for use on the Grimsby & Immingham. The last cars over the routes were No 62 to Saltwell Park and No 60 to Bensham. The latter featured as the last car at the next conversion when, on 7 April 1951, the route to Low Fell was converted to bus operation. At this stage the chairman of Northern General, W. T. James, estimated the cost of replacing the trams was £350,000.

The penultimate route converted was that to Teams, which succumbed on 14 July 1951. The final abandonment occurred on 4 August 1951 with the route to Dunston converted to bus operation. The final service car, No 20, left Newcastle Central station at 11.00 pm; this was followed by No 16, repainted for the occasion, on which the official closure party travelled for the final journey. Following closure, No 52 was preserved locally (it became part of the TMS

The last car to serve Bensham on 3 March 1951 was 1921-built No 60, seen here at the route's terminus. Tony Wickens/Online Transport Archive (489)

No 60 was again used on 7 April 1951 when the route to Low Fell was converted to bus operation. Tony Wickens/Online Transport Archive (542)

collection in 1960) and a further batch of single-deck cars – 1, 3/4, 7-11/14/16/17, 56,58-60/ – was sold to British Railways. Of these, No 4 was damaged beyond economic repair while being unloaded and No 6 replaced No 14 as the latter had a motor problem. The ex-Gateshead cars

Gateshead No 52 stands at the terminus of the Teams route. This service was converted to bus operation on 14 July 1951, the penultimate conversion in Gateshead.
R. W. A. Jones/Online Transport Archive (GD13)

continued to operate over the Grimsby & Immingham until it closed in 1961; on withdrawal Nos 5 and 10 were preserved.

Gateshead Depot

Gateshead & District Tramways Co Ltd was operated out of a single depot, Sunderland Road, which was located on the route east towards Heworth. The depot opened in 1883 to house the company's steam trams with the electric cars arriving in 1901. The depot ceased to house trams with the final closure of the system in August 1951; the adjacent yard – where new sidings had been added in 1950 for the purpose – was then used for the scrapping of those trams not sold to Grimsby or preserved.

Gateshead Closures
16 April 1948
Low Fell via Central Station-Gosforth

5 March 1950
Wrekenton-Heworth

3 March 1951
Saltwell Park-Bensham

7 April 1951
Low Fell

14 July 1951
Teams

4 August 1951
Dunston

Gateshead Fleet

1-20

Built between 1920 and 1928, these twenty single-deck trams were fitted with bodies supplied from Gateshead's own workshops with the exception of Nos 1 and twenty, which were supplied by Brush. All were fully enclosed from new with the exception of Nos 13/15 (of 1920/21), which were rebuilt as fully enclosed in 1926/27. The first four built – Nos 12/13/15/19 – were fitted with Brill 22E trucks, and the remainder received Brill 21Es. All withdrawn between 1947 and 1951, Nos 1, 3-11/16-18, 20 were sold for reuse on the Grimsby & Immingham, although No 4 was damaged on delivery and never entered service. Nos 5 and 10 were preserved in 1961 following final withdrawal.

21-23/26-28, 32/34/39-41/43/44

In 1901 Gateshead acquired a batch of twenty-five open-top double-deck cars, Nos 21-45, that were fitted with ER&TCW bodies on Brill 21E trucks when new. Those cars that survived in 1945 had been rebuilt with open-balcony top decks in 1924/25. The remainder were scrapped and their trucks reused on the second-hand trams acquired from Liverpool and Sheffield. The post-war

Numerically the first of the twenty single-deck cars supplied to Gateshead & District between 1920 and 1928, No 1, is seen here at the terminus of the Bensham route. No 1 was one of the cars sold for further service on the Grimsby & Immingham line following withdrawal on Tyneside. Gateshead was unusual in permitting advertising on tramcar rocker panels. R. W. A. Jones/Online Transport Archive (GD6)

survivors were all withdrawn between 1947 and 1951.

24/25, 33/36/37

Dating originally to 1899 when they were supplied to Sheffield Corporation – Nos 16, 35/37/38, 74 (the actual order of renumbering is uncertain) – these five cars were built with open-top bodies supplied by G. F. Milnes & Co (Nos 16, 35/37/38) and ER&TCW (No 74) on Brill

No 27, seen here at Saltwell Park, was one of twenty-five double-deck cars that had originally been delivered as open-top four-wheel cars in 1901. Those cars, like No 27, that survived into the post-war era had received open-balcony top covers in the mid-1920s. Gateshead was the last major system that had significant section of single track with passing loops. R. W. A. Jones/Online Transport Archive

21E trucks. Fitted with open-balcony tops in Sheffield, the five cars were sold to Gateshead, where lower-deck vestibules were fitted, in 1922. Withdrawal took place during 1950 and 1951. Although not preserved at the time, part of the body of No 33 was subsequently rescued and restored at the National Tramway Museum as Sheffield No 74.

In 1922, Gateshead acquired five cars second-hand from Sheffield; originally new in 1899, the cars had received their open-balcony tops before purchase by Gateshead. One of the five, No 33, is recorded at the Museum in Newcastle on 4 March 1950. Although not preserved when withdrawn, the body of No 33 was later rescued and has been restored as Sheffield No 74 at the National Tramway Museum.
John Meredith/Online Transport Archive (101/8)

29, 30/38

These three cars were originally Liverpool Nos 479-81 respectively and were acquired by Gateshead in 1921. Constructed in 1899 with open-top bodies supplied from Liverpool's own workshops on Brill 21E four-wheel trucks, the three trams were rebuilt as fully enclosed in 1925. The three cars were withdrawn during 1950 and 1951.

31/35, 42

Built in 1902 for Sheffield Corporation – Nos 176/82/86 respectively – these three trams were originally fitted with open-top bodies built by Cravens on Brill 21E four-

wheel trucks. Acquired by Gateshead in 1922, the trio had had open-balcony bodies fitted in Sheffield and had lower-deck vestibules added by Gateshead. All three were withdrawn between 1946 and 1951.

45

This was one of a batch of open-top double-deck trams, Nos 21-45, that had been supplied with ER&TCW bodies on Brill 21E four-wheel trucks in 1901. No 45's survival was due to the fact that it had been converted to a small single-decker in 1923, when it was also renumbered from No 25. It was latterly used as a snowplough and survived until withdrawal in 1947.

46-50

Delivered in 1902 as open-vestibule single-deck combination cars fitted with Milnes bodies on Milnes trucks, these five cars had the open smoking compartments enclosed in 1907, and became fully enclosed during 1931 and 1932. All were retrucked between 1921 and 1925 with

One of the sextet of ex-Oldham trams, No 35, stands at the Wrekenton terminus on 26 February 1950. No 35 had originally been Oldham No 24 when new in 1924.
Tony Wickens/Online Transport Archive (264)

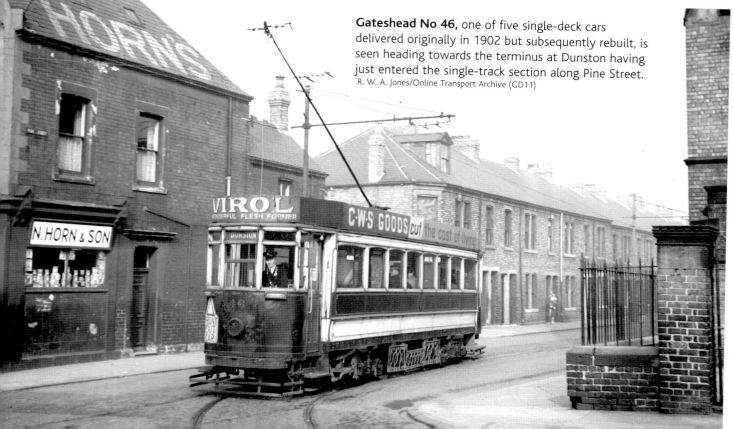

Gateshead No 46, one of five single-deck cars delivered originally in 1902 but subsequently rebuilt, is seen heading towards the terminus at Dunston having just entered the single-track section along Pine Street.
R. W. A. Jones/Online Transport Archive (GD11)

Gateshead No 51 is believed to have been delivered as an open-top double-deck car in 1901 by ER&TCW, but had been converted to single-deck and given a longer – 8ft 0in – Brill 21E truck to replace its original 6ft 0in wheelbase one. Originally numbered 45, it became No 51 in 1925. *Harry Luff/Online Transport Archive (T300)*

Brill 22E four-wheel trucks reused from the original batch of Nos 11-20. The five cars were withdrawn in 1947.

51

Traditionally this has been regarded as another atypical survivor of the batch of open-top cars supplied in 1901. According to this narrative, No 51 was originally numbered 45 and had been renumbered in 1925 after being rebuilt as a small single-deck car in about 1920. It survived until the system's closure when it was rescued, without motors, for preservation. The body of the car survived – in an increasingly dilapidated condition – until rescued by the Beamish Museum, County Durham, with a view towards eventual restoration. However, research on the recovered body suggests that this traditional story might not be accurate as the body of the supposed No 51 shows considerable detail differences to that of car No 51 when in service.

52

This was originally numbered 7 when built in 1901 as one of a batch of cars, Nos 1-10, that was supplied with ER&TCW single-deck California-style bodies on Brill 21E four-wheel trucks. The car was rebuilt, following a fatal accident, as a single-deck saloon tram in 1920 – although little of the original car was used – and was renumbered in the late 1920s when new trams numbered 1-20 were supplied to the operator. As non-standard the car was used in its latter days on the route to Teams, although it could occasionally be found on the Dunston and Bensham routes. No 52 was withdrawn in 1951 and subsequently preserved

In its later years, No 52 was regularly used on the service to Teams and it is on this route that the car is illustrated here. No 52 had had an eventful life by the date of its withdrawal; it was rebuilt from a California-style single-deck car in 1920 following an accident on Bensham Road in which four pedestrians were killed, and nine passengers and the conductress were injured. *R. W. A. Jones/Online Transport Archive (GD12)*

privately; it was part of the National Tramway Museum collection. Ownership of the tram has passed to Beamish. Now stored at Beamish, plans are in place restore the car to an operational condition.

53

Built in 1907, with a body constructed in Gateshead's workshops on Brill 22E bogies, No 53 was rebuilt in 1926 and remained in service until withdrawal in 1947.

54/55

These two cars were built in 1913 with single-deck bodies constructed in Gateshead's own workshops on Brill 39E

bogies. The pair were withdrawn for scrap in 1947 having been rebuilt in 1926.

56-60

In 1921 Gateshead & District acquired a batch of five cars with Brush-built single-deck bodies on Brill 38E bogies. Following withdrawal in 1951, the five cars were sold for further service on the Grimsby & Immingham, where they operated until 1961.

61-67

This batch of seven fully enclosed trams supplied in 1923 were the last wholly double-deck new trams that Gateshead & District acquired. Fitted with Brush-built bodies on Brill 21E four-wheel trucks, the

Gateshead No 54 was one of two single-deck cars delivered in 1913. It is pictured at Gateshead West station on 4 March 1950.
John Meredith/Online Transport Archive (100/12)

Gateshead No 60 was one of a batch of five single-deck cars delivered in 1921. Like the other four, No 60 was sold to British Railways for use on the Grimsby & Immingham line on withdrawal in 1951.
Geoffrey F. Ashwell/Online Transport Archive

No 67, seen here at the Saltwell Park terminus, was the last of the seven fully enclosed Brush-built cars supplied to Gateshead & District in 1923. The BET 'wheel and magnet' logo is evident above the lower-deck windows.
R. W. A. Jones/Online Transport Archive (GD10)

With two Newcastle trolleybuses in the background, one of Gateshead's six ex-Oldham cars, No 71 (originally Oldham No 18), is recorded at the junction of Pilgrim Street and Market Street in central Newcastle on 4 March 1950.
John Meredith/Online Transport Archive (101/4)

seven cars remained unmodified during their operational career and survived until withdrawal in 1951.

35, 68-72

In 1946 Gateshead & District acquired six trams from Oldham; these were originally Oldham Nos 24, 122/25/28, 18 and 17, respectively, and had been new in 1924 (Nos 35, 71 and 72) and 1926 (Nos 68-70). The first to enter service was No 68 in early 1947, with the last being No 35. All were fitted with English Electric-built fully enclosed bodies on Brill 21E four-wheel trucks. The six remained in service until 1951.

In 1948 Gateshead & District took advantage of withdrawals in Newcastle to purchase five trams from its northern neighbour. No 74 was the second of the batch and had been originally Newcastle No 43; it is pictured here at Low Fell. All five survived until 1951 with Gateshead & District.
R. W. A. Jones/Online Transport Archive (GD4)

73-77

These five trams were acquired second-hand from Newcastle in 1948 and had been numbered Nos 80, 43, 54, 88 and 52 respectively by their original owner. Dating to 1901, the trams were initially fitted with single-deck bodies built by Hurst Nelson on Brill 27G bogies, but the majority were later rebuilt between 1916 and 1927 with enclosed vestibules. A number of the cars, including those sold to Gateshead, were fitted with replacement Peckham P25 bogies. The five cars survived with Gateshead & District until 1951.

HULL

ollowing the closures of 1940 and 1942, Hull retained only a single tram route – route D from Osborne Street to Dairycoates (which represented the curtailment of the Hessle Road route with the outer section abandoned following the co-ordination agreement with East Yorkshire Motor Services in 1934) – and even this single route would only just see peace restored in Europe. On 30 June 1945 this final route closed when the last service car, No 105, departed the city centre at 10.20 pm to be followed at 10.40 pm by No 169. Suitably illuminated for the occasion, No

169 carried the lord mayor, the sheriff and other dignitaries while being crewed by two aldermen. At closure, services were provided by eighteen double-deck trams, which were sold to Leeds following withdrawal.

Hull Depot

Hull entered the Second World War with two surviving tramway depots. However, the reduction in the fleet following the wartime closures of the routes along Holderness Road (17 February 1940) and Anlaby Road (5 September 1942) permitted

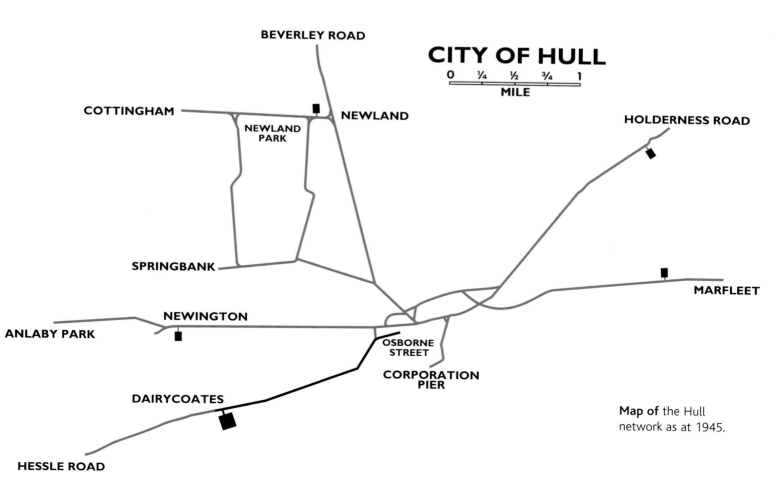

Map of the Hull network as at 1945.

One of Hull's fleet, No 111, is pictured at the Dairycoates terminus. The signal in the foreground controlled the level crossing immediately in front of the tram. Originally the route stretched beyond Dairycoates to Hessle, but this section was converted to bus operation before the war.
J. H. Roberts/Online Transport Archive

Hull No 169, suitably bedecked for the occasion, was used for the final journey on Hull's tram system on 30 June 1945. Seen here, posed before or after the final trip, the car was crewed by two of the city's aldermen.
Barry Cross Collection/Online Transport Archive

the transfer of thirty-two trams to Leeds and the closure of Wheeler Street as a tram depot at the same time as the Anlaby Road trams were withdrawn. The single remaining depot, Liverpool Street (which also served as the main workshops), was closed as a tram depot with the closure of the system on 30 June 1945.

Hull Closure

30 June 1945
Osborne Street-Dairycoates

Hull Fleet

103/05/11/13

These four cars were the survivors of a batch of 15, Nos 102-16, supplied with Milnes bodies on Brill 21E trucks. Although originally open-top, open-balcony top covers were fitted before entry into service in 1903. All were rebuilt as fully enclosed between 1920 and 1931. A number of the

batch – Nos 104/09/14-16 – were sold to Leeds in 1942. The surviving cars were all withdrawn in June 1945 and sold, with the exception of No 103, to Leeds.

117/19

The surviving examples of a batch of six delivered in 1909, Nos 117/19 were fitted with UEC bodies on M&G 21EM trucks originally. No 117 received a Brill 21E truck in the early 1930s. Originally a batch of open-balcony cars, the trams were rebuilt as fully enclosed between 1933 and 1935 using top decks salvaged from withdrawn cars. Both survived until June 1945 when No 117 was sold to Leeds for further service.

123

No 123 was the first of fourteen open-balcony cars delivered in 1909/10 that were fitted with bodies supplied from the

Hull No 111 was one of four from a batch supplied in 1903 that survived into 1945. It is seen here in 1945 shortly before the system's abandonment at the city terminus, Osborne Street, of the one surviving route. Evidence of damage from the Luftwaffe attacks on the city and its important docks is evident. J. H. Roberts/ Online Transport Archive

Hull No 176, recorded here at Dairycoates in front of the depot, was one of five surviving members of a batch of twenty delivered in 1915. These five, plus three sold to Leeds in 1942, were rebuilt as fully enclosed between 1933 and 1935. Of the five survivors, only one (No 173) was sold to Leeds following the closure of the Hull system.
J. H. Roberts/Online Transport Archive

corporation's own workshops on M&G 21EM four-wheel bogies. All were rebuilt as fully enclosed between 1920 and 1931, and Nos 124-36 were sold to Leeds in 1942. Upon withdrawal in 1945, No 123 was also sold to Leeds. No 132 was preserved following withdrawal in Leeds; it is currently on display in Hull on long-term loan from the National Tramway Museum.

139/42/46/48/51/60

These six cars were the survivors of a batch of twenty-four open-balcony cars, Nos 137-160, supplied in 1912. They

were fitted with Brush bodies on Brill 21E trucks and all, with the exception of Nos 137/41/57, were rebuilt as fully enclosed between 1933 and 1935 using top decks salvaged from withdrawn cars. A number – Nos 138-40/42/47/50/52-56/58-60 – were sold to Leeds following withdrawal in 1942 and 1945.

169/70/73/75/76

The surviving examples of a class of twenty – Nos 161-80 – delivered in 1915, these cars were originally fitted with open-balcony Brush bodies on Brill 21E four-wheel trucks. Nos 163/64/69/70/73-76 were rebuilt as fully enclosed between 1933 and 1935 using top decks salvaged from withdrawn trams. Nos 163/64/74 were sold to Leeds in 1942 with No 173 following in 1945.

LEEDS

eeds could lay claim, via the Roundhay operation that started in November 1891, to be a pioneer of electric trams powered via the overhead. Although there had been a number of route closures during the 1930s, these were all the routes outside the city boundary – following a decision taken in 1932 – and the bulk of those routes within the city that were predominantly single track with loops. These closures dramatically improved the financial position of the transport department and were, to an extent, countered by the opening of extensions.

Work continued on improving the network as late as 1942 with the doubling of the Compton Road route. The fleet had also undergone considerable modernisation, with the construction of the 100 'Horsfield' cars in 1931/32, the 17 'Middleton Bogies' in 1933-35 and the three four-wheel cars, Nos 272-74, in 1935. At the outbreak of war in September 1939, the vast bulk of the fleet was less than 20 years old. Most may have been traditional four-wheel cars but regular fleet modernisation had ensured the trams still had many years of useful service in them.

Much of the development of the

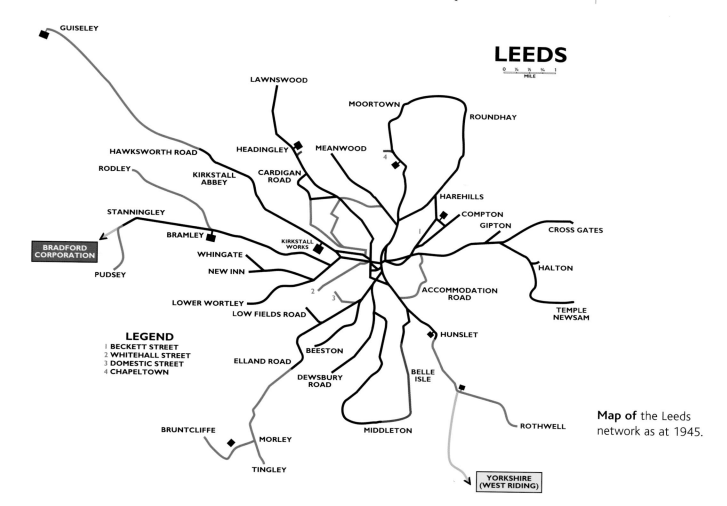

Map of the Leeds network as at 1945.

LEEDS

0 ¼ ½ ¾ 1
MILE

LEGEND
1 BECKETT STREET
2 WHITEHALL STREET
3 DOMESTIC STREET
4 CHAPELTOWN

GUISELEY
LAWNSWOOD
MOORTOWN
ROUNDHAY
HAWKSWORTH ROAD
HEADINGLEY
MEANWOOD
RODLEY
KIRKSTALL ABBEY
CARDIGAN ROAD
HAREHILLS
STANNINGLEY
COMPTON
GIPTON
CROSS GATES
BRAMLEY
KIRKSTALL WORKS
BRADFORD CORPORATION
WHINGATE
HALTON
PUDSEY
NEW INN
LOWER WORTLEY
ACCOMMODATION ROAD
LOW FIELDS ROAD
TEMPLE NEWSAM
HUNSLET
BEESTON
ELLAND ROAD
BELLE ISLE
DEWSBURY ROAD
BRUNTCLIFFE
MORLEY
MIDDLETON
ROTHWELL
TINGLEY
YORKSHIRE (WEST RIDING)

In 1949 a new terminal stub was constructed at St Chad's, Headingley, to replace the life-expired crossover at West Park; with the southern wall of Headingley Depot forming a backdrop, 'Pilcher' No 281 stands on the St Chad's stub awaiting its next duty.
R. W. A. Jones/Online Transport Archive (LS32)

Leeds system during the 1930s was the result of the management of W. Vane Morland, appointed in 1932. The Leeds system emerged from the Second World War with its fleet supplemented by the acquisition of second-hand trams from Hull, and of single-deck Sunderland No 85, along with ambitious plans for tramway development including the construction of subways to serve the central area. This latter project was announced in November 1944 by the city council and followed on from Vane Morland's two reports to the Reconstruction Committee produced in April and June 1944. Vane Morland recognised that street tramways in the central area might have to be reduced, but he saw subways as a means of retaining this form of transport. Authority had been

granted in 1941 for the extension of the Belle Isle route, which had been opened as far as Belle Isle circus on 22 July 1940, and this was confirmed in 1945; work started on the extension and the first half-mile was opened on 24 February 1946, while work continued on the eventual link through to Middleton.

At the end of the war there remained three sections of route that were predominantly single track and, in furtherance of the pre-war policy, these sections were quickly converted to bus operation. The routes affected were the 11 – Harehills via Beckett Street – and the 19 – to Lower Wortley – both of which were converted on 25 August 1946, and the section of the 27 beyond Hyde Park to Cardigan Road that survived until 7 December 1947. Following the conversion of the 11 in August 1946, through services were introduced between Gipton and Dewsbury Road, a revision that brought the ex-Hull cars to York Road for the first time. The Gipton service, route 21, was renumbered 11 as from 15 September 1946. Apart from these abandonments, five sections of line over which no regular services operated also disappeared; these were: Reginald Terrace (12 November 1944), Marsh Lane to Kirkgate (former inward line, 19 November 1944), St Pauls Street to Westgate (29 October 1945), Stanley Road (4 February 1946) and Infirmary Street (22 September 1946).

Fleet changes in the immediate post-war period were relatively limited. The second batch of ex-Hull cars was delivered following that system's closure on 30 June, and the conversions of August 1946 and December 1947 did not result in significant withdrawals. The early post-war years witnessed some withdrawals, most notably the bulk of the surviving balcony cars and the first of the ex-Hull cars (Nos 471/76), but the first of the ex-Manchester cars (No 287) entered service on 3 August 1946. Initially this car emerged in a grey livery but with Leeds' coat of arms and destination blinds. Another change saw the introduction of paper or painted adverts, which resulted in the end of lining out on the upper-deck panels. A number of the 'Chamberlain' cars received replacement P35 trucks that were built by the corporation itself at Kirkstall under licence from Brush.

During 1947, work was undertaken on the track with relaying undertaken in Meadow Lane, Burmantofts Road, Headingley and Boar Lane, and with new terminal stubs being constructed at Stainbeck Lane (Chapeltown, opened 1948), Haddon Road (Kirkstall Road) and St Chads Road (Headingley, built to replace the life-expired crossover at West Park, opened early 1949). Late 1948 saw work in hand relaying the Dewsbury Road route and on work

In 1948 the corporation decided to restore one of the surviving 'Balcony' cars, No 309, for film use and possible preservation; in the event, No 328 was restored – as No 309 – and is seen here in its post-restoration condition. Unfortunately, when withdrawn in 1951, there were no parties willing to take it on for preservation and the car was consequently scrapped.
Barry Cross Collection/Online Transport Archive

towards the completion of the Belle Isle to Middleton extension. The latter saw a slightly premature passenger journey when an inexperienced driver mistook the Belle Isle terminus and proceeded a short distance over the new route. The extension opened in two stages in 1949 – on 6 March, when No 164 in the pale blue livery was the first car to use the new line, and 28 August, when No 268 was the first car to carry passengers on the new circular route via Middleton (route 12) and No 271 the first via Belle Isle (the 26) – thus completing the circle. The completion of the route marked the final extension to the Leeds network.

On the vehicle front No 276, eventually the only all-new four-wheel car to enter service in Leeds post-war, was officially

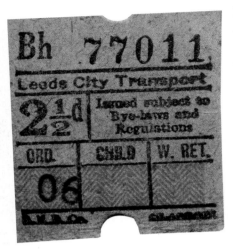

Leeds Corporation introduced the Ultimate type of ticketing equipment to trams on 16 December 1948. They were first used on the corporation's buses three years later. This is an example from the first style of tickets by GNP.
Author's Collection

launched on 15 September 1948 and entered public service five days later. One of the three ex-London Transport 'HR/2' cars acquired pre-war emerged in June 1948 in a modified version of the pale blue livery that adorned 'special' cars in place of the more usual deep blue; the period witnessed a considerable experimentation in livery treatment. Also in 1948 the chief engineer, V. J. Matterface, introduced a complex system of car classification so that, for example, the 'Middleton Bogies' became Classes D2 (Brush-built) or D3 (English Electric-built). In early 1948 there was a renumbering of certain trams: Nos 275, 176 (original), 105, 321, 332 and 287 became Nos 349, 342, 275, 337, 338 and 280 respectively. No 280 emerged with its new number repainted in the standard dark blue livery. Between September and December 1948 a further six ex-Manchester trams, Nos 281-86, entered service in a revised paler blue livery with silver roof. Nos 281 and 282 were initially used on the Roundhay/Moortown/Lawnswood routes, but complaints from passengers over the quality of the ride led them to be transferred to Swinegate Depot for use on lines with less reserved track. Originally it had been decided to restore No 309 for possible preservation; however, No 328 was in better condition and the two cars swapped identity. The new No 309 reappeared in the fleet's old brown and yellow livery, and was used for film and other work. In this guise it survived until 1951 when, with more expenditure required, it was offered for potential preservation. There were no takers, unfortunately, and the car made its one-way journey to Cohen's scrapyard in October 1951.

On 18 January 1949 it was decided that the section of line between Kirkstall

Abbey and Hawksworth Road would be converted to bus operation. The reason was that the track was in a poor condition and would cost £43,000 to repair for a section that carried relatively little traffic. It was also agreed not to take further a proposed half-mile extension to the Horsforth route as the corporation did not wish to operate trams outside the city's boundary (indeed, many of the pre-war abandonments had been to withdraw services beyond the boundaries). On 30 January 1949 Bramley Depot was closed to permit its conversion into a bus garage; to accommodate the displaced trams a line previously occupied by works cars at Swinegate was used and a second siding installed.

December 1948 saw a further change with the introduction of the Ultimate ticket system; this was introduced initially on vehicles at Headingley and Chapeltown depots, although it was found unsuitable for use on Nos 272-74; as a result Nos 272-74 were transferred to Swinegate and No 273 was sent to Kirkstall for reseating used second-hand seats from Bradford. All tram services operated using the Ultimate system by the end of 1950, although the conversion of the city's bus services took longer. More trams were, by this date, appearing in a lighter blue livery and the decision was made that, in the future, fleet numbers would be displayed using the simpler Gill Sans typeface. Relaying was undertaken on the Middleton route and along Corporation Road, although the rarely used curve in City Square linking Infirmary Street with Park Road was removed. On 6 June 1949 the first of the ex-Southampton cars, No 290, entered service in the light blue livery; it had been repainted in Southampton before heading north, but had undergone a full overhaul at Kirkstall before entering service. In all, eleven ex-Southampton cars entered service; a further twenty-six were acquired, but their poor condition

meant that all were ultimately scrapped either in Leeds or Southampton without entering service in Leeds. The cost of the first six had been £135 apiece. The majority entered service in the new royal blue livery, the standard livery from 3 July 1949, although No 299 emerged in the new red livery on 20 October 1950, and the last, No 300, entered service on 16 December 1950 in the dark blue livery. In September 1949 London No 2099 was transferred to Leeds where it operated for a period with its London Transport fleet

number. The acquisition of the 'Feltham' cars had become practical as a result of work undertaken to realign a number of junctions with a view to the operation of 44ft-long bogie cars as part of the subway plan.

In late 1949 Vane Morland was replaced by A. B. Findlay as general manager. Findlay had been rolling stock engineer in Glasgow, involved in the design of that city's more modern trams and was thus ideally qualified to take further, in theory, Leeds' progressive

Still bearing its London Transport fleet number but adorned with Leeds Corporation crests, 'Feltham' No 2099, the first of the type to reach Leeds, is pictured on the track through Middleton woods during a TLRS tour on 11 June 1950.
John Meredith/Online Transport Archive (120/11)

views for tramway development. In reality, however, the tide turned against the trams and projects, such as the three single-deck cars (Nos 600-02), did not prevent the elimination of the network. That sentiment was gradually turning against the tram was evinced in late 1949 when the city's chief constable, I. W. Barnet, advocated the removal of trams from Boar Lane to relieve congestion. This proposal was rejected by the Transport Committee and its chairman, Councillor J. Rafferty, who suggested that congestion could be reduced by more parking restrictions and the redirection of less essential traffic away from Boar Lane.

The first contraction occurred on 3 December 1949 when, despite opposition (and a petition with 1,434 names), trams were withdrawn from the Kirkstall Abbey to Hawksworth Road section. More positive was the decision in early 1950 to acquire ninety-two of the 'Feltham' cars then being withdrawn by London Transport; the cost of each car was £500. The 'Felthams' would be allocated to Torre Road Depot, and used initially on the routes to Crossgates, Halton, New Inn, Temple Newsam and Whingate. These trams were too long for the traverser at Kirkstall Works and so a new direct line was installed to permit the 'Felthams' direct access to the paint shop. Perhaps as a result of the red that No 2099 operated in when first in Leeds, the decision was taken in early 1950 that the royal blue livery, adopted as standard only in the summer of 1949, would be replaced by red for the trams and green for the bus fleet.

On 15 April 1950 Kirkstall Works ceased to be a running depot for buses; thereafter it was primarily used for the maintenance of the tram fleet until the abandonment process resulted in it ceasing to do such work in November 1957 (when the work for the system's last two years was transferred to Swinegate). At about the same time, there was a fleet reallocation between the four operational tram depots. All trams were based at Swinegate with the following exceptions: Chapeltown: Nos 51-70, 201-10, 423-32; Headingley: 71-92, 211-16/72-74/76/77/92/93; Torre Road: 93-103/05-42, 259-54/91, 443-45, 2099.

On 26 June 1950 the *Blackpool Evening Gazette* reported that the chairman of the Leeds' Transport Committee, Councillor J. Rafferty, along with his vice chairman, Alderman Cowling, and general manager, A. B. Findlay, had visited Blackpool to drive one of that operator's PCC cars and that there was the possibility of a vehicle loan to Leeds in view of the city's interest in operating modern single-deck cars. Although the loan did not take place, the visit undoubtedly influenced the design of Nos 601/02. The summer of 1950 also saw the introduction of the new standard red and cream livery; there were a number of experimental variants before a final version, with subtle differences to accommodate the differences in the various tram bodies, was settled on in October 1950. One of the variants was 'Feltham' No 502, which emerged from Kirkstall Works in a striking red, green and white livery; this did not, however, last long. Among the first cars to emerge in the new red livery were the first of the 'Felthams' then being transferred from London. As the new 'Felthams' arrived at Torre Road, they displaced 'Chamberlains' to Swinegate that, in turn, saw a number of older cars – most notably the ex-Hull cars – withdrawn. Subsequent 'Felthams' saw Nos 501-20 transferred to Swinegate as the type's area of operation expanded. The Beeston route was, however, barred to the type. No 2099 was returned to service on 3 August 1950 renumbered 501, but still retaining its London Transport livery following minor work at Kirkstall Works; these included the fitting of side indicator blinds.

At this stage, eleven ex-Hull trams remained in service with eight others awaiting scrapping. The 'Beeston Air Brakes' were to be withdrawn when a major overhaul was required. On 30 September 1950 the Whingate service was renumbered 15. It was understood that no further tram routes were to be converted to bus operation; the short Hunslet route had been considered at risk, but the relaying of its junction with the Belle Isle route indicated that this was not the case. By early 1951, thirty-one 'Felthams' had been received with sixteen in service; withdrawn ex-Hull and Hamilton cars were having their bodies burnt at the siding on Low Fields Road with their equipment being sold for further use to Calcutta.

On 21 January 1951 the short working of the Lawnswood route at West Park was revised to terminate at the ring road. Also in January 1951 'Feltham' No 517 emerged experimentally with a pantograph as opposed to the usual bow collector; three more, Nos 528-30, emerged in service during March 1951 also fitted with pantographs. The experiment, however, was not deemed a success and the pantographs were removed in June 1951 following an incident when the pantograph fouled a spanwire outside the Majestic Cinema. At the time it was suggested that the removal was temporary pending the realignment of the overhead, but this was never undertaken. In February 1951 'HR/2' No 278 was fitted with airbrakes to see if the surviving examples then in service with LT could be so fitted; the Ministry of Transport would only agree to the sale of these cars if they could be so fitted, and both Glasgow and Leeds were possibly interested. Neither proceeded with a purchase. No 278 was subsequently allocated to Chapeltown depot.

By 15 April 1951, fifty-four 'Felthams'

In early 1951 'Feltham' No 517, seen here on a service towards Crossgates, emerged into service with a pantograph rather than the more usual bow collector; this was one of four of the type so treated experimentally. Following an accident, the pantographs were removed during the summer. Barry Cross Collection/Online Transport Archive

had been received with thirty-five in service. Their arrival permitted the withdrawal of the remaining ex-Hull cars, the rebuilt balcony cars, the 'Hamilton' air-braked cars, all bar two of the 'Pivotals' (Nos 396 and 408), two of the 'Pilchers' and five of the ex-Southampton cars. By the summer sixty 'Felthams' had made the journey north along with ex-LT No 1 (which became Leeds No 301), which was sent in lieu of two 'Felthams' – Nos 2144/62 – that had been destroyed by fire in London before being sent to Leeds. On 23 July 1951 the part-day service from Beeston to Swinegate was diverted to operate over Sovereign Street rather than Swinegate and Neville Street; this was the only service to operate over the single-track Sovereign Street section.

By the end of 1951 all the ex-MET 'Felthams', Nos 501-50, were in service and the first of the ex-LUT examples, No 551, was due to enter service on 26 October. The last of the type to reach Leeds, LT No 2158, reached the city on 6 October 1951. By 20 October a number of older cars had been scrapped at Low Fields siding; these included No 309, the balcony car restored earlier with a view to possible preservation. By the summer of 1952, twenty 'Felthams' were allocated to Swinegate for use on the Hunslet, Belle Isle and Dewsbury Road services. A total of sixty-eight of the type had entered service by the end of May that year but, it was reported, the remainder were stored at Torre Road with no work being undertaken. Withdrawals following the introduction of the later 'Felthams' included two 'Pilchers' and No 377; the tram fleet now numbered 396 of which about 100 remained in the old blue livery. On 15 August 1952 the Victoria Road spur on route 27 was replaced by a lengthened crossover at Hyde Park. On 4 September 1952 an accident occurred when No 507 ran away at Roundhay and collided with No 92, injuring twelve including three members of staff. No 92

was so seriously damaged that it was withdrawn immediately and No 507 was not repaired, formally being taken out of service on 28 July 1953. The official Ministry of Transport enquiry concluded that the driver had failed to use the handbrake and that conductors should be better informed about emergency braking procedures.

Although the trams were still relatively secure, there were straws in the wind that indicated all was not well. The economics of tramway operation had deteriorated – track, for example, had more than doubled in price per tonne since the end of the war – and, although there had been fare increases and service alterations (such as on 18 August 1952 when the Hyde Park-Belle Isle service had been reduced to peak hours and Saturdays only), the financial position was poor. On 30 January 1953 the *Yorkshire Evening News* published the first of three articles advocating tramway conversion. Although the articles were subsequently condemned by the lord mayor, Alderman Frank Burnley, local politics were to play their part as the Labour Party went into the local elections of 1953 advocating conversion with the Conservative Party arguing for retention. With the Labour Party retaining control, the tramways' future was doubtful. On 14 June 1953 the Transport Committee agreed to convert the Kirkstall and Stanningley routes, the two biggest loss makers, to bus operation.

On 4 October 1953 the Stanningley route, the 14 from Corn Exchange to Half Mile Lane (the short section from Half Mile Lane to Cohen's Foundry having been abandoned on 2 January 1953 without replacement), was converted to bus operation. Some twenty-four trams were withdrawn as a result. Work proceeded rapidly to recover the overhead, which had only recently been replaced in part for reuse elsewhere, and the terminal loop at Corn Exchange was also removed as it had only been used for the 14. Although the system was now under threat, work had resumed in preparing some of the remaining stored 'Felthams' for use and the first of the new single-deck cars entered service, the latter in a special purple livery to mark the coronation of HM Queen Elizabeth II.

Following the conversion, the Transport Committee, chaired by the anti-tram Labour councillor J. Rafferty, decided, despite the opposition of the Conservative group led by Councillor Mather, on 16 November 1953 that the entire system was to be converted to bus operation over the next ten years. By the end of 1953 the tram fleet had been reduced to 338 passenger cars. On 7 March 1954 the short working on route 4 at Haddon Place was abandoned to permit the construction of a new bus turning loop; this foreshadowed the conversion of route 4 to Kirkstall Abbey to bus on 4 April 1954; also converted at this date was route 10 to Compton Road. Trams continued to operate along Kirkstall Road as far as the main workshops for a further three years.

The section beyond Kirkstall Abbey to Hawksworth Road had been abandoned without replacement on 3 December 1949; between then and 3 April 1954 the route terminated at Kirkstall Abbey near where 'Horsfield' No 222 is pictured. R. W. A. Jones/Online Transport Archive (LS70)

Following these conversions, trams on the Dewsbury Road route now operated through to Harehills and Roundhay (via Briggate) as route 3, or to Gipton as

No 425, seen here at the Compton Road terminus, was one of a batch of thirty-five 'Chamberlain' cars delivered between 1926 and 1928; the service to Compton Road was replaced by buses on 3 April 1954. R. W. A. Jones/Online Transport Archive (LS43)

Leeds No 600 is seen under construction in Kirkstall Works; converted from Sunderland No 85, which had been acquired by Leeds in late 1944, No 600 was the last of the three new single-deck cars to enter service. By its introduction, however, the tide had turned against the tram in Leeds and No 600 eked out its short life largely on the Hunslet service.
R. W. A. Jones/Online Transport Archive (LS20)

long gone and the three cars eked out their existence on the short route until withdrawal.

In early 1955 the first of the outstanding 'Felthams', Nos 570/80, entered service; these were followed between then and July 1956 by a further thirteen. The last was No 582 on 31 July 1956; this was also the last 'new' tram to enter service in Leeds. The remaining seven cars, Leeds Nos 571/72/75-78/84, were scrapped without use between 5 July 1956 and 9 November 1956.

The next route conversion occurred on 24 April 1955 when the 11 to Gipton succumbed; this involved 605 yards of double track that had, before the war, been seen as the basis of an extension – never completed – into the Seacroft estate. At the same time Chapeltown ceased to be an operational depot, although a number of works cars were stored in the depot thereafter. This conversion was followed on 25 June 1955 by the conversion of two routes. These were routes 6 from Corn Exchange to Meanwood and 8 from Corn Exchange to Elland Road (which operated as a through service); the Low Fields Road branch, last used for football specials on 3 May 1955, was cut back to the scrapyard. The section beyond the football ground to the greyhound stadium had been abandoned without replacement during

route 11. With the closure of Headingley depot, the Lawnswood route was now served by cars from either Swinegate or Chapeltown. Withdrawn at this stage were the last 'Pilchers' and the final 'Pivotal'.

On 4 August 1954 the last of the single-deck cars, No 600, finally entered service; allocated to the Hunslet route – where it was soon to be joined by Nos 601/02 – the dream of a network of subways had

The Gipton route, once planned to be extended into the Seacroft estate, was converted to bus operation on 24 April 1955. A car heads from the terminus along the extension to Gipton that had originally opened on 11 September 1936. R. W. A. Jones/Online Transport Archive (LS19)

Another casualty of 1955 was the service to Elland Road, which was converted to bus operation on 25 June. Here 'Horsfield' No 242 stands at the original Elland Road terminus showing a through service to Meanwood on route 6. Services from here to the football ground were withdrawn without replacement in 1954. Originally, corporation services operated south of this point to Tingley and Bruntcliffe, but these routes had been abandoned in 1935. R. W. A. Jones/Online Transport Archive (LS24)

The route to Beeston was converted to bus operation on 19 November 1955. Seen in the company of one of the corporation's fleet of works cars – plus trailer – is 'Horsfield' No 194 awaiting departure from the Beeston terminus with a service to the Corn Exchange. The route to Beeston was cut back slightly in 1941 to this terminal point. Phil Tatt/Online Transport Archive (1058)

No 281, one of the ex-Manchester Corporation 'Pilcher' cars, stands at the Lawnswood terminus with a service heading towards Moortown via the city centre. By this date No 281 had been fitted with an EMB Hornless four-wheel truck. Following the conversion of the route via Headingley to Lawnswood on 3 March 1956, the circular services (2/3) were linked with the Dewsbury Road service.
R. W. A. Jones/Online Transport Archive (LS51)

1954. The conversion of routes 6 and 8 permitted the withdrawal of thirty-four cars. From 26 June 1955 cars on route 5 to Beeston terminated at the Corn Exchange, being extended to Harehills during peak hours; by this date, these cars were the only trams to use the northern part of Vicar Lane. With Councillor Rafferty now advocating a more rapid conversion programme, an application was made to convert the Beeston route; this was duly granted and route 5 was converted to bus operation on 19 November 1955. During late 1955 work was undertaken at Swinegate to increase its capacity to permit the removal of the remaining trams from Torre Road. Among the withdrawals following the conversion of

the Beeston route were Nos 272-74, the three 'Lance Corporals' built in 1935.

At the start of 1956 the passenger fleet comprised 287 cars: 69 'Chamberlains', 103 'Horsfields', 17 'Middleton Bogies', Nos 275/76, 3 'HR/2s', No 301, 89 'Felthams' (of which 77 were in service) and the three single-deckers. There were also twelve works cars and three ex-passengers in use as works cars. The next conversion occurred on 3 March 1956 with the removal of trams on route 1 from City Square via Headingley to Lawnswood. The last car to Lawnswood was 'Horsfield' No 225. From this date Moortown (route 2) was linked with Dewsbury Road (route 9), with additional cars from Dewsbury Road running to

The route to New Inn was converted to bus operation on 21 July 1956. Here 'Feltham' No 532 stands at the New Inn terminus awaiting its next duty. R. W. A. Jones/Online Transport Archive (LS23)

Harehills and Roundhay (route 3) during busy periods. The part-day service from Hyde Park to Belle Isle was also withdrawn with all cars to Belle Isle now running to Swinegate. These changes resulted in the withdrawal of a number of 'Chamberlains' and 'Horsfields', and

work for Nos 600-02 was also reduced following the greater integration between the Belle Isle and Hunslet services.

The next conversion occurred on 21 July 1956 with buses replacing trams to New Inn (16) and Whingate (route 15); from the same date, services to

Also converted to bus operation on 21 July 1956 was the service to Whingate. 'Feltham' No 525, another of the ex-MET batch, is pictured at the terminus at Whingate. Phil Tatt/Online Transport Archive (1087)

R. W. A. Jones/Online Transport Archive (L22)

The Whingate and New Inn routes split at the junction of Tong Road and Whingate; heading inbound, having just departed from New Inn, 'Feltham' No 586, one of the ex-LUT cars, approaches the junction with the Whingate route.

Middleton were linked with the services along York Road; these changes resulted in 'Feltham' cars being used regularly on the Middleton route for the first time. The conversion of routes 15 and 16 resulted in the end of passenger cars using City Square; thereafter, until 8 November 1957 when all work was transferred to Swinegate, the only trams to use City Square were those heading to or from Kirkstall Works. Following this conversion, the last 'Chamberlains' were withdrawn along with three more of the 'Middleton Bogies'; only six of the latter – Nos 257/61/62/65/68/69 – remained in service. With No 582 entering service, the fleet now stood at 173 with a further 50, mostly destined for scrap, in store. In late 1956 the junction with Harehills Road and Roundhay Road, which represented the stub of the long-closed route 11 via Beckett Street, which had been retained as a siding, was lifted. Also in late 1956 the scrapyard at Low Fields Road was leased to Messrs Standish; work in recent months had included the

scrapping of many 'Chamberlains' along with a number of 'Middleton Bogies' and those 'Felthams' that had never entered service. Withdrawals during the period saw the final 'Chamberlains' taken out of service along with 'Middleton Bogies' Nos 265 and 269; the first of the 'HR/2s', No 277, that succumbed after an accident; and seven 'Felthams' (Nos 552/55/71/72/75/79/84). The stock now comprised 170 trams, of which 157 were in service.

Late 1956 witnessed the onset of the Suez Crisis, following Britain and France's failed invasion, and the decision was made not to undertake any further conversions during the emergency. Indeed, football specials to Elland Road for first and second team matches were reintroduced, first running on 8 December 1956. This required the reactivation of the junction with the Dewsbury Road route. The reintroduced specials operated until 16 March 1957. Track on the Hunslet route received attention; had it not been for the crisis, trams would have been

One of the Brush-built 'Chamberlain' class, No 22, is pictured on Dewsbury Road. The Dewsbury Road route was converted to bus operation on 28 September 1957. R. W. A. Jones/Online Transport Archive (LS13)

The Roundhay, via Chapeltown, service was converted to bus on 28 September 1957. Here one of the three streamlined four-wheel cars of 1935, No 274, heads past Chapeltown Library with a service to Roundhay. Immediately in front of the tram can be seen the junction for the terminal stub in Stainbeck Lane that was added in 1948. R. W. A. Jones/Online Transport Archive (LS33)

'Chamberlain' No 39 passes inbound from Lawnswood through City Square with a Roundhay via Harehills circular; this section of City Square was abandoned in March 1956.
Phil Tatt/Online Transport Archive

removed from the route earlier; the planned closure of the Moortown and Dewsbury Road routes, planned for March 1957, was also deferred.

However, once the crisis eased, the process of conversion resumed. In spring 1957, forty-one trams, including the 'HR/2s', the remaining 'Middleton Bogies' and four 'Horsfields', were offered for sale for scrap. The track in Vicar Lane, which had been retained following the conversion of route 5 in 1955 for possible diversionary use, was partially covered over. The next conversions occurred on 28 September 1957, with the

conversion of Route 2 to Moortown via Chapeltown and Route 9 to Dewsbury Road to bus operation. This resulted in the end of the circular route 2/3 via Roundhay and Moortown; thereafter cars serving Moortown via Roundhay displayed route 3 in both directions. The junction for the Dewsbury Road route at Moor Road was quickly replaced by plain track and the section of line along Swinegate itself was no longer required. With the withdrawals resulting from these conversions, including the final 'Middleton Bogie' (No 268), the fleet was reduced to 135 of which 25 were

The circular routes via Middleton – the 12 and the 26 via Moor Road and Belle Isle respectively – were converted to bus operation on 28 March 1959. The route via Belle Isle included the only substantial post-war extension to the Leeds system. Seen passing at Middleton are two of the 'Middleton Bogies', Nos 265 and 269, which had been withdrawn in late 1956. R. W. A. Jones/Online Transport Archive (LS41)

not in service. All surviving service cars were either 'Horsfields' or 'Felthams'; ex-LT No 301 was also withdrawn in September 1957 and passed to the BTC for preservation – it was collected for preservation on 26 November 1957. On 8 November Kirkstall Works ceased to handle tramcar repairs with work transferred to Swinegate; this permitted the closure of the section of track through City Square to the Works. Truck work, however, continued at Kirkstall with any trucks requiring maintenance moved to the Works by road. The first two cars to receive attention at Swinegate were Nos 194 and 568. Swinegate also undertook the repainting of trams, releasing one per week on average through to July 1958 when the last two, Nos 153/54, were completed.

Although there were no conversions during 1958 the fleet was reduced slightly, but on 28 March 1959, three services were converted to bus operation: route 3 from Briggate to Moortown; route 12 from City to Middleton via Moor Road; and route 26 from City to Middleton via Belle Isle – this included the section of line only completed in 1949. The last

trams from Moortown were Nos 171, 160 and, with civic dignitaries on board, No 192. The last cars on routes 12 and 26 were Nos 167 and 526 respectively; when they crossed on the post-war extension, photographs were taken. With these conversions, the York Road routes now terminated at Kirkgate and the fleet size was more than halved as fifty-five trams were withdrawn. It was estimated that the remaining services required no more than forty cars: fifteen 'Felthams' and twenty-five 'Horsfields'.

On 18 April 1959 route 25 to Hunslet was converted to bus operation; this meant no trams now operated south of the city centre and the decision was made to advance the final conversion from 3 January 1960 to 7 November 1959. Following the Hunslet conversion, the maximum fleet requirement was twenty-six, although twenty-seven 'Horsfields'

The short route to Hunslet was converted to bus operation on 18 April 1959. For some years this route had been the haunt of the three single-deckers, but their use declined until withdrawal in 1957. Here 'Feltham' No 502 is seen at the terminus before heading back towards Swingate.
Phil Tatt/Online Transport Archive (1072)

One of the four routes, all served by the York Road corridor, to survive until the final closure, Halton was served by a short branch off the route to Temple Newsam. Here 'Feltham' No 547 is seen descending Halton Hill. The section of line down Halton Hill had been doubled during the 1930s. Phil Tatt/Online Transport Archive (1040)

The Temple Newsam service terminated in woodland close to the city's museum; here a car on route 22 awaits departure from the route's sylvan terminus.
R. W. A. Jones/Online Transport Archive (LS17)

and nineteen 'Felthams' still remained operational. The final closure was not long in coming. On 7 November, after almost seventy years, Leeds bade farewell to electric trams. The last passenger car to Temple Newsam, at 4.20 pm, was No 531; the last to Halton, at 4.38 pm, was No 158; and the last to Cross Gates, at 4.39 pm, was No 181. No 181 was the last car in passenger service, returning to Corn Exchange at 5.30 pm. At 6.15 pm the closing convoy left Swinegate depot comprising of ten 'Horsfields' with a decorated No 178 leading. This was followed by Nos 173/76/89/75/91/98/71/72/60 (with No 160 also decorated accommodating tramway pensioners) as far as the junction between the Cross Gates and Temple Newsam routes diverged; the first five, led by No 170, headed for Cross Gates with the second five, led by No 191, heading for Temple Newsam. The two batches then headed back to Swinegate with No 178 being the last to arrive at 7.16 pm.

Following the closure, work proceeded to scrap in Swinegate all the remaining cars that were not designated as possible preservation candidates. By 31 January 1960, two 'Horsfields' (Nos 160 and 202) remained at Swinegate; both were scheduled for preservation, but both were later scrapped. There were also fifteen 'Felthams', including two for preservation (Nos 517/26), along with the three single-deck cars. The remaining cars destined for scrap were soon dealt with, leaving Swinegate depot to accommodate Nos 202, 526, 600-02 pending removal inside and Nos 160 and 517 outside, along with tower wagon No 1 and rail grinder No 6. The latter four had been acquired by Leeds University Railway Society and were destined to move to the Middleton Railway for preservation.

Leeds Depots

As might be expected with a network of its size, Leeds had a number of tram depots operational between 1945 and closure in 1959. Indeed the facilities had been improved considerably during the 1930s with the construction of the new depot at Torre Road, which opened in 1938 and was extended a couple of years later with a second shed and yard, and the expansion of Swinegate earlier in the decade. The corporation's main workshops were at Kirkstall Road, which had also been a running shed until 1931. Tramway work ceased at Kirkstall on 8 November 1957. The operational depots in Leeds were as follows: Bramley, built on Stanningley Road at the junction between the Stanningley and Rodley routes, was the first tram depot to close post-war when it succumbed on 30 January 1949 to be converted into a bus garage; Headingley depot, sited on Otley Road, lost its tram allocation on 3 April 1954; Chapeltown, located on Harrogate Road on the circular route via Moortown, lost its tramcar allocation on 23 April 1955, although it stored withdrawn trams thereafter; Torre Road, sited on York Road, accommodated trams until 19 November 1955; and Swinegate, situated on Sovereign Street directly south of Wellington and New station, survived until the system's final closure on 7 November 1959, having taken over the maintenance of the tram fleet in November 1957 following the cessation of that work at Kirkstall.

Leeds Closures

Note: a number of routes were cross-city and route numbers changed according to direction of travel.

24 August 1946
11 – Nipper Lane-Beckett Street, Stanley Road and Harehills Road
19 – Crown-Lower Wortley

7 December 1947
27 – Victoria Road and Cardigan Road

3 December 1949
4 – Kirkstall Abbey-Hawksworth Road

2 January 1953
14 – Half Mile Lane-Stanningley

3 April 1954
4 – City Square-Kirkstall Abbey
10 – York Road-Compton

24 April 1955
11 – Corn Exchange-Gipton

25 June 1955
8 – City to Elland Road/Lowfields Road
6 – City-Meanwood

19 November 1955
5 – City Square-Beeston

3 March 1956
1 – City Square-Lawnswood

21 July 1956
15/16 – Briggate-Whingate/New Inn

28 September 1957
2 – City-Moortown (via Chapeltown)
9 – City-Dewsbury Road

28 March 1959
3 – Briggate-Moortown (via Harehills)
12 – City-Middleton (via Moor Road)
26 – City-Middleton (via Belle Isle)

18 April 1959
25 – Swinegate-Hunslet

7 November 1959
17 – City-Harehills Lane;
18 – City-Cross Gates; 20 – City-Halton;
22 – City-Temple Newsam

Leeds Fleet

1-75

The seventy-five 'Chamberlain' cars were delivered during 1926 and 1927. They were fitted with fully enclosed bodies supplied by Brush on EMB Pivotal four-wheel trucks. Nos 1-4, 6-10/12, 34/38/39, 44/49, 51-57/59, 60/62/64/65/67/68, 71-4 received replacement Peckham P35 trucks during the period between

One of the Brush-built 'Chamberlain' class, No 3, is pictured at the terminus of the Gipton route. This was one of sevnty-five cars built by Brush in 1926 and 1927. The last were withdrawn from service in 1956. Phil Tatt/Online Transport Archive (1081)

1946 and 1949. In November 1959 Nos 1 and 9 exchanged numbers. No 57 was renumbered 64 in December 1955 and, in January 1956, 141. Nos 80 and 96 swapped numbers in September 1955. No 81 was renumbered 142 in January 1956. All the class was withdrawn for scrap between 1951 and 1956.

76-103/05-50

Further 'Chamberlain' cars Nos 76-150 were also delivered during 1926 and 1927, but were fitted with English Electric bodies again on EMB Pivotal trucks. All bar Nos 85/86, 97/98, 104/17-19/21/27/ 29/33/44/46/48/50 received replacement Peckham P35 trucks between 1945 and 1952. No 104 was withdrawn in 1942. Nos 102/112 exchanged numbers in November 1955. The new No 102 exchanged numbers with No 115 in February 1956. No 141 was renumbered 64 in January 1956. No 142 was renumbered 135 in December 1955. No 83, withdrawn in November 1955, was

The second batch of 'Chamberlain' cars, Nos 76-150, was supplied by English Electric. No 131, seen here at Temple Newsam, was one of the batch that received a replacement Peckham P35 truck between 1945 and 1952. The route to Temple Newsam featured a section of roadside right of way through the estate, and served the parkland and Jacobean mansion that had been acquired by the corporation in 1922. Temple Newsam House serves as one of Leeds' museums and is widely regarded as one of the finest non-national collections in the country. R. W. A. Jones/Online Transport Archive (LS18)

During the Second World War, the corporation built a single four-wheel car; this was 'Austerity' No 104, which became No 275 in 1948. In its later guise, the car is seen on route 14 at the Little King Street crossover on Wellington Street on 11 June 1950.
John Meredith/Online Transport Archive (120/7)

converted into snowplough No 7 and was finally withdrawn in 1959. All the type were withdrawn for scrap between 1952 and 1956.

104

This was a single 'Austerity' four-wheel car built in 1943 at Kirkstall Works on a Peckham P35 truck. It initially took the number of the sole 'Chamberlain' car withdrawn during the war but was renumbered 275 (ii) in 1948. It remained in service until 1957.

115A/17A/18A/20A/22A/23A, 275/76 (i)

During 1908 and 1909 Leeds took delivery of a batch of 12 open-balcony four-wheel trams with bodies built at Kirkstall Works on Brill 21E trucks. The cars were all renumbered with an 'A' suffix in 1927. During 1938 and 1939 Nos 119A and 124A

were rebuilt and renumbered Nos 275/76. These two cars were again renumbered, to 342/49 respectively, in 1948. The six unrebuilt survivors were withdrawn in 1945, and Nos 342 and 349 remained in service until 1949 and 1951 respectively.

151-54

These four trams were the prototypes of the 'Horsfield' cars and were constructed in Kirkstall Works with fully enclosed bodies on Peckham P35 (Nos 151/52/54) or EMB Flexible (No 153) trucks in 1930. All four survived until withdrawal in 1958 and 1959.

155-254

Following on from the construction of the four prototype 'Horsfield' or 'Showboat' cars, 100 four-wheel trams were supplied with Brush bodies during 1931 and

In 1930 Leeds Corporation constructed four prototype cars, Nos 151-54, in Kirkstall Works; these were the forerunners of the successful 'Horsfield' cars delivered over the following two years. The first of the quartet, No 151, is recorded at Harehills.
R. W. A. Jones/Online Transport Archive (LS21)

1932. All were fitted with Peckham P35 trucks, although No 174 operated with an   EMB Hornless between 1950 and 1954, and No 201 with an M&T Hornless between 1945 and 1951. No 179 operated with an ex-Liverpool EMB Hornless truck (which had previously been used on No 396) between 1950 and 1954. Nos 180/89 exchanged numbers in April 1958; 212/42 and Nos 219/21 did the same in December

Following on from the delivery of four prototype cars in 1930, a further 100 four-wheel 'Horsfield' or 'Showboat' trams were delivered during 1931 and 1932. A. C. Crichton/Hamish Stevenson Collection/Online Transport Archive

One of the eight 'Middleton Bogies' built by English Electric, No 269, is pictured on Swinegate. All were withdrawn by the end of 1957, and it is regrettable that none of this stylish class survived into preservation.
R. W. A. Jones/Online Transport Archive (LS9)

1957. The 'Horsfields' were withdrawn between 1957 and 1959; No 189 was preserved and restored as No 180, its original number, as part of the National Tramway Museum collection. Nos 160 and 202 were also initially preserved, but were subsequently scrapped.

255-71

These seventeen bogie cars, the 'Middleton Bogies', were supplied with Brush (Nos 255-63) or English Electric (Nos 264-71) bodies on M&T Swing-link bogies. The Brush-built cars were delivered between 1933 and 1935, and those by English Electric in 1935. All were withdrawn for scrap during 1956 and 1957.

272-74

Nicknamed the 'Lance Corporals' as a result of the V-shaped band below the vestibule window, these three four-wheel cars were built in Kirkstall Works on M&T Swing-link trucks in 1935. All three were withdrawn in 1954 and 1955 and subsequently scrapped.

277-79

In 1939 Leeds acquired three 'HR/2' class trams from the London Passenger Transport Board. Originally delivered to the London County Council in 1930, the three cars were fitted with Hurst Nelson bodies on EMB Heavyweight bogies. Nos 277-79 were numbered 1881/83/86 respectively in London. In February 1951

Three four-wheel cars were built at Kirkstall Works in 1935. Nos 272-74 were nicknamed 'Lance Corporals' as a result of the V-shaped band at either end. The last of the trio, No 274, is seen in City Square on a service to Roundhay via Harehills.
R. W. A. Jones/Online Transport Archive (LS4)

No 278, which also included the fitting of platform doors, showed that the equipment could be fitted, but the cost meant no further cars were converted; apart from one preserved example (No 1858) the remaining London 'HR/2s' were scrapped. Nos 277-79 remained in service in Yorkshire until 1957.

283-90/92 (i)

These nine cars were delivered as open-balcony cars in 1911-12. The tenth car of the batch, No 291, was withdrawn in 1940 and dismantled. Fitted with bodies built at Kirkstall Works, the ten were originally fitted with UEC Spring yoke flexible four-wheel trucks; the latter, however, were short-lived with six of the cars receiving Brill 21E trucks in 1913-14 and the remaining four in 1919. The cars, which were fitted with reverse staircases, retained their open balconies until withdrawal; the surviving nine cars were all taken out of service by the end of 1945.

280-87 (ii)

Leeds was one of four operators to acquire Manchester 'Pilcher' cars during the late 1940s when they were being withdrawn in Lancashire. Delivered originally between 1930 and 1932, the eight cars were fitted with Manchester-built bodies on Peckham P35 trucks, Nos 280-87 entered service between 1946 and 1948, and were Manchester Nos 287, 104, 272/66, 144, 263 and 370 respectively. No 287 initially retained its Manchester number until renumbered 280 in 1948. No 282 received a replacement EMB Hornless truck in 1951. All seven were withdrawn between 1952 and 1954, and were scrapped.

293-301 (i), 302-12/14-69

These open-balcony cars were built at Kirkstall Road Works between 1913 and 1923. As built, all were supplied

Leeds No 277, seen in excellent external condition on the Moortown route, was one of a trio of LPTB 'HR/2' trams acquired second-hand in 1939. Nos 277-79 remained in service in the West Riding until 1957.
R. W. A. Jones/Online Transport Archive (LS5)

No 278 was fitted experimentally with M&T air-wheel brakes to supplement its existing equipment. Both Leeds and Glasgow had expressed interest in acquiring the surviving 'HR/2' cars as they were withdrawn in London. However, the Ministry of Transport would not sanction the sale unless the cars were fitted with air brakes and so the work was undertaken on No 278 to see if it was practical. The work on

with either Brill or Hurst Nelson 21E trucks, although Nos 293-97 were later fitted with Brush trucks and Nos 360-69 with Peckham P22s. Nos 294, 312/330-39 were fitted with Hurst Nelson 21E trucks in 1945; No 339 was subsequently fitted with a Peckham P22 truck in November 1948. A number of the cars – Nos 321/32/39-41/43-69 – were fully enclosed between 1935 and 1937, except No 339 that was so treated in March 1942; these were known as 'Convert' cars. No 313 was withdrawn and dismantled in 1940. In 1948 fully enclosed Nos 321 and

Leeds, along with Aberdeen, Edinburgh and Sunderland, took advantage of the abandonment of the tramways in Manchester to acquire a batch of the 'Pilcher' cars that dated originally to the early 1930s. Leeds acquired eight, Nos 280-87, that entered service between 1946 and 1948. The second of the batch, No 281 (originally Manchester No 104), is pictured in City Square heading towards Chapeltown.
R. W. A. Jones/Online Transport Archive (LS12)

332 were renumbered 337 and 338 respectively, and surviving open-balcony car No 328 was renumbered 309 and restored to its pre-war livery for filming purposes. Although the new No 309 was intended to be preserved, it was scrapped on withdrawal. The survivors were withdrawn between 1944 and 1951.

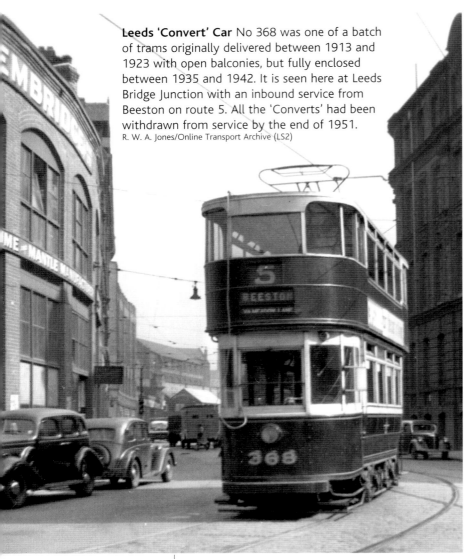

Leeds 'Convert' Car No 368 was one of a batch of trams originally delivered between 1913 and 1923 with open balconies, but fully enclosed between 1935 and 1942. It is seen here at Leeds Bridge Junction with an inbound service from Beeston on route 5. All the 'Converts' had been withdrawn from service by the end of 1951.
R. W. A. Jones/Online Transport Archive (LS2)

No 345, withdrawn in 1948, survived, however, until the final closure of the Leeds system in 1959 in use as a joinery store and was subsequently preserved; it has been fully restored as a 'Convert' car at the National Tramway Museum.

276 (ii)

The final four-wheel double-deck car built for Leeds, No 276 was constructed in Kirkstall Works on a Peckham P35 truck in 1948 as the prototype for a new class. No further new double-deck trams were, however, completed. No 276 was withdrawn for scrap in 1957.

290-300 (ii)

In 1949 Leeds took advantage of the closure of the Southampton system to acquire a number of fully enclosed four-wheel cars that dated originally to 1929-32. Eleven of the cars, Nos 290-300, entered service; these had been Southampton Nos 108/09/07/06/05/04, 50, 35/32, 25/23 respectively. Nos 301-08/10-12 were allocated to a further 11 cars that were also delivered to Leeds but never entered service. A further nine were also acquired, but scrapped in Southampton. All had bodies built by

Although Leeds acquired a number of second-hand double-deck trams both during and after the Second World War, only one wholly new double-deck car was built post-war – No 276. This car was constructed in 1948 and is seen here on Dewsbury Road.
Harry Luff/Online Transport Archive

Southampton Corporation on Peckham P35 trucks. Those that entered service were withdrawn during 1952 and 1953 for scrap; ironically the remains of those that did not enter service lasted longer, only being scrapped in 1958.

301

Two of the 'Feltham' trams acquired by Leeds – Nos 2144/62 – failed to make it to Yorkshire and, in their place, the experimental London County Council No 1 of 1932 came northwards. This had a body built by LCC on EMB Heavyweight

With the imposing lines of the Queens Hotel behind it, ex-Southampton car No 297 stands in City Square with a service to Hyde Park. A total of eleven ex-Southampton cars, with their familiar roof profile (to permit operation through the Bargate in their home city), entered service in Leeds in 1949. Plans to place additional cars in service came to nothing and those that did enter service had only a relatively short life in Yorkshire, all being withdrawn by the end of 1953. The Queens Hotel, designed for the London, Midland & Scottish Railway by W. Curtis Green and W. H. Hamlyn, was constructed in 1937. R. W. A. Jones/Online Transport Archive (LS10)

bogies. Nicknamed 'Bluebird' when built as a result of its non-standard livery, No 301 was sold to Leeds in 1951. It remained in service with Leeds until 1957. Preserved on withdrawal, it now forms

part of the National Tramway Museum collection, having been restored back to London Transport condition.

370-92

Delivered between 1923 and 1925, these cars fitted with bodies built at Kirkstall Road Works were the first Leeds trams to be delivered fully enclosed. All were fitted with Peckham P22 trucks when new but Nos 389 and 392 were fitted with Peckham P35 and Cravens trucks respectively in 1925, and No 393 was fitted with a Peckham P22 two years later. Nos 370-76 were the last trams delivered to Leeds fitted with reverse staircases. The cars were withdrawn from service between 1949 and 1952, the last survivors being Nos 375/77.

393-99, 401-410

Delivered during 1925 and 1926, with the final five cars (Nos 406-10) following in 1928, these fully enclosed four-wheel

The unique ex-London Transport car, by now renumbered Leeds No 301, is seen in City Square while operating on the Moortown circular route.
Harry Luff/Online Transport Archive (T879)

Leeds No 375 was one of the last two survivors of twenty-three cars, Nos 370-92, that were built at Kirkstall Works between 1923 and 1925. It was also one of the last trams delivered to the corporation with reversed stairs.
Barry Cross Collection/ Online Transport Archive

Originally one of fourteen cars supplied during 1925 and 1926 that were fitted with EMB Pivotal trucks, by 10 June 1950, when No 396 was photographed at Kirkstall Abbey, the car had received a replacement EMB Hornless truck acquired second-hand from Liverpool. Ultimately No 396 was the last of the 'Pivotal' cars to remain in passenger service, although No 399 survived in works use and was subsequently preserved.
John Meredith/Online Transport Archive (120/5)

cars were supplied with bodies from Kirkstall Road Works. Nos 393-98 and 403-10 were originally supplied with EMB Pivotal trucks, and Nos 399 and 401/02 had Peckham P22 trucks. Nos 393 and 402 were subsequently converted to Peckham P22 trucks. In January 1950 No 396 was fitted with an ex-Liverpool EMB flexible truck; this was exchanged with a Peckham P35 truck from 'Horsfield' No 179 in March of the same year. All were withdrawn between 1950 and 1954, the last survivor being No 396. Following withdrawal, No 399 was used as the works' shunter and survived into preservation; it has now been fully restored at the National Tramway

Museum as the only surviving 'Beeston Air Brake' – it was one of a number of the type fitted with air brakes in the mid-1920s to operate over the steep track to Beeston.

400

Built in 1925, this was the prototype for the 'Chamberlain' cars (1-150, 411-45) and was delivered with a fully enclosed body supplied by Kirkstall Road Works that differed from the bodies supplied to those on the 394-99/401-10 batch in having no upper-deck bulkheads. It was fitted with an EMB Pivotal four-wheel truck. Chamberlain wished to introduce route numbers; as a result, this was the

Leeds No 400
was the prototype
of the 185
'Chamberlain' cars
delivered between
1926 and 1928, and
was built in Kirkstall
Road Works in
1925. It survived
in service until late
1951.
J. Joyce Collection/Online
Transport Archive

first car delivered that had provision for
route number boxes at both ends. No 400
remained in service until withdrawal in
October 1951.

411-45

These thirty-five were a further batch of
'Chamberlain' trams, and were delivered
between 1926 and 1928. Built with fully
enclosed bodies at Kirkstall Works on
EMB Pivotal trucks, Nos 420/23/33/39
received replacement Peckham P35
trucks between 1945 and 1949. All were
withdrawn between 1951 and 1955. On
withdrawal in 1953, No 420 became open-
top tower wagon No 2, surviving until
1959.

446-487

In 1942 and 1945 Leeds acquired two
batches of trams second-hand from
Hull; thirty-two, Nos 446-477, came in
1942 with the remainder coming in 1945
following the abandonment of the Hull
system. They were originally Hull Nos
132, 127, 130, 26, 136, 126, 129, 124, 128,
133, 125, 131, 135, 115, 134, 150, 159, 153,
147, 156, 155, 109, 174, 152, 116, 114, 138,
154, 163, 164, 158, 104 respectively as the
first batch and Nos 142, 140, 105, 139, 123,
113, 111, 117, 160 and 173 in 1945. All –
with the exception of No 26 (built in 1927)
and 113 (built in 1925) – were originally
open-balcony cars built between 1903 and
1915 that had been fitted with enclosed

The first significant acquisition of second-hand trams by Leeds saw forty-two four-wheel cars move from Hull to the city in two stages in 1942 and 1945. Leeds No 457, originally Hull No 131 and seen here in Swinegate, was one of the first batch to arrive. All were destined to have a relatively short life in Leeds, with all being withdrawn by 1951.
R. W. A. Jones/Online Transport Archive (LS7)

balconies between 1920 and 1932. The cars supplied to Leeds were among those that had been retrucked and remotored in Hull during the 1930s; Nos 446-58, 460-63/68, 472-75/79, 481/82/86/87 were fitted with Peckham P22 trucks and the remainder with Brill 21Es. The first cars withdrawn were Nos 471 and 476, which succumbed in 1946; the remainder were withdrawn between 1949 and 1951. One of the ex-Hull cars, No 446 (ex-Hull No 132) was preserved and is now on display in its home city. Apart from these cars, Leeds also acquired Hull No 96 in 1942. This was a single-deck stores and snowplough car that had been converted from an open-top Hurst Nelson car of 1901 in 1933. This car was also preserved on withdrawal and, converted to a single-deck passenger car, is now used at the Heaton Park tramway in Manchester.

501-590

In 1949 Leeds acquired London Transport Executive 'Feltham' No 2099; for a brief period this car operated in Leeds wearing its London number. Between then and

The most significant addition to the Leeds fleet in the post-war years was represented by the acquisition of a number of the 'Feltham' class of bogie trams as they were withdrawn in London. In all, ninety of the class headed to the West Riding, but the winds of change were reaching Leeds as well and, eventually, not all of the ninety that Leeds received entered service. One of the ex-Metropolitan Electric Tramways cars, No 541, is seen at Halton.
R. W. A. Jones/Online Transport Archive (LS15)

The three single-deck cars, with No 600 closest to the camera, are pictured in Swinegate Depot on 1 November 1959 awaiting their fate. No 600 was acquired from Sunderland in 1944, but it never operated in original condition in Leeds, but was rebuilt between 1949 and 1954 as part of the still-born project to construct tram subways in the city. Although all three cars were initially preserved, No 601 was subsequently scrapped as a result of vandalism on the Middleton Railway.
John Meredith/Online Transport Archive (431/8)

1951 a further eighty-nine 'Felthams' were sent northwards. Nos 501-50 were ex-Metropolitan Electric Tramway cars, and Nos 551-90 were ex-London United Tramways. All had been built by Union Construction & Finance Co of Feltham in Middlesex and dated to 1930/31. The ex-MET cars were fitted with EMB Maximum Traction bogies, and ex-LUT cars had English Electric bogies. Nos 501-50 had originally been LTE Nos 2099/97/77/82/69/66/70/73/78/74, 2105, 2085, 2100/15, 2093/80, 2118, 2087/84/81/72, 2108, 2096,/76/83/85/75/86, 2116, 2071, 2106/04, 2092, 2102/19/10, 2089/94/68, 2114/07, 2098/05/90, 2111/01/12/03/17 and 2079, and 551-90 had been LTE Nos 2139/64/50/38/31/52/20/21/37/48/25/61/40/23/26/34/36/37/32/41/55/28/24/29/56/51/45/42/46/49/43/33/60/35/59/57/47/53/54/58. Each 'Feltham' cost £500 and underwent overhaul at Kirkstall before entering service; the ex-MET cars were classified 'UCC/1' and the ex-LUT examples 'UCC/2'. All the ex-MET cars entered service, but Nos 571/72/75-78/84 of the ex-LUT batch were ultimately scrapped without service in Leeds. In August 1957 Nos 505 and 20 swapped

numbers as did Nos 511 and 519. Nos 517/54 swapped numbers in February 1959 as did Nos 524/65 in November 1958. Nos 527/28 swapped numbers in July 1957 and the new 528 exchanged numbers with No 538 in August 1957. No 582 was the last tram to enter service in Leeds – on 31 July 1956. Nos 557/64 exchanged numbers in February 1959 as did Nos 561/87 the same month. No 507 was withdrawn following an accident in 1952. The remainder of the ex-MET cars were withdrawn between 1957 and 1959; two – Leeds Nos 501/26 – were preserved. The former, now restored to London Transport condition, is part of the London Transport Museum collection; the latter is still in Leeds livery in an unrestored condition at the Seashore museum in the USA. Withdrawal of the ex-LUT 'Felthams' took place between 1956 and 1959; ex-No 554 was initially preserved but, following vandalism, was scrapped in 1968.

600

In November 1944 Leeds acquired Sunderland single-deck No 85, but it never entered service. Renumbered 288 in 1948, the tram was rebuilt in Kirkstall Works between 1949 and 1954 as the third of the experimental single-deck trams; it entered service on 4 August 1954 at a time when closure was now policy and the first significant route abandonments had taken place. No 600 was used, along with Nos 601/02, largely on the Hunslet service, where the three single-deck cars were adequate for the route. Withdrawn in 1957, No 600 remained in stock at the end of the system and was subsequently preserved; it now forms part of the National Tramway Museum collection.

601/02

The Leeds-based bus bodybuilder Charles H. Roe supplied two bodies in 1953 – the only tramcar bodies built by the company – to Leeds for the construction of two

new single-deck trams. Designed as the forerunners for a modern fleet of trams to operate through the proposed city-centre subways, No 601 was fitted with EMB Lightweight bogies, and No 602 received M&T PCC bogies and VAMBAC; the former cost £12,000 and the latter £13,000 – both considerably more than the cost of a contemporary double-deck bus. Both entered service in a special purple livery to mark the Coronation of HM Queen Elizabeth II. The changed environment meant plans for the tram subways were abandoned and these two cars, along

In 1953, the Leeds-based manufacturer Charles H. Roe supplied two modern single-deck trams to the corporation – the last wholly new trams built for it. No 601, seen here at the Hunslet terminus, was the more conventional of the two, being fitted with normal control equipment. Never destined to be used to their full potential, the railcars eked out their existence until withdrawal. No 601 was preserved upon withdrawal, but was scrapped following vandalism on the Middleton Railway.
Phil Tatt/Online Transport Archive (PTP1)

Leeds Corporation works car No 4a was converted in 1936 from an ER&TCW car, No 256, that had originally been delivered in 1902. Numbered 3 when first converted, the car was renumbered 4a in 1948.
Marcus Eavis/Online Transport Archive

with No 600, were never used to their full capabilities. Nos 601 and 602 both succumbed in 1957 and were preserved; unfortunately the former, after suffering damage on the Middleton Railway, was scrapped, although No 602 survives as part of the National Tramway Museum collection.

Works Cars

Leeds Corporation employed a significant fleet of dedicated works cars. A number were built specifically for works duties, but others were converted

from redundant passenger cars. One of the fleet was acquired second-hand from Hull Corporation in 1942; this was No 6 (originally Hull No 96), which was preserved on withdrawal and is now part of the collection at Heaton Park. A second preserved works tram is rail derrick No 2, which was built in 1953 and now forms part of the National Tramway Museum Collection at Crich.

NEWCASTLE

ollowing decisions made in the early 1930s, about half of the city's tramcar network had been converted to bus and trolleybus operation and, by 1945, the network had contracted effectively to the routes north and east of the city with the exception of the long route west to Throckley. To operate this network, 220 trams survived, the newest of which dated from 1926.

Even before hostilities ceased, an application was made to the Ministry of War Transport to operate trolleybuses over the remaining routes, including those across the Tyne to Gateshead.

Formal powers to convert the remaining network were covered by the Newcastle-upon-Tyne (Trolley Vehicles) Order Confirmation Act of 1945, which reconfirmed the powers to operate trolleybuses over the Tyne bridges (although only one short section of this Act was actually completed; the Act stipulated that Newcastle Corporation would pay for all the costs of wiring the High Level and Tyne bridges), and the Newcastle-upon-Tyne Corporation Act of 1946, which was passed despite objections from Gateshead & District, Tyneside Tramways & Tramroads Co and

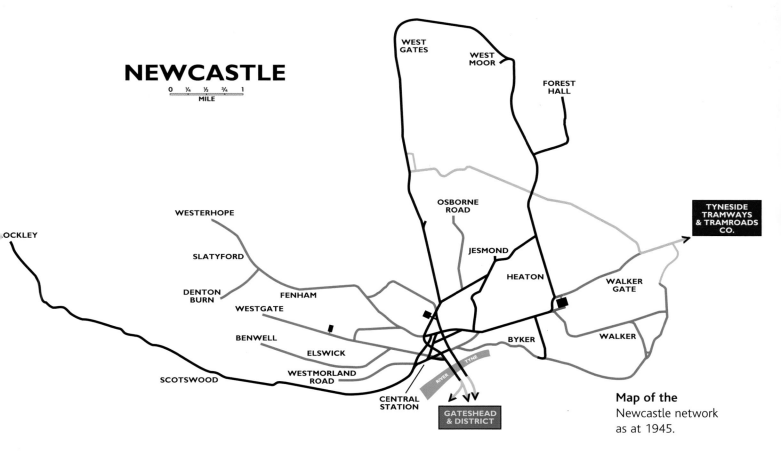

NEWCASTLE

0 ¼ ½ ¾ 1
MILE

WEST GATES

WEST MOOR

FOREST HALL

WESTERHOPE

OSBORNE ROAD

TYNESIDE TRAMWAYS & TRAMROADS CO.

OCKLEY

SLATYFORD

JESMOND

HEATON

WALKER GATE

DENTON BURN

FENHAM

WESTGATE

BENWELL

ELSWICK

BYKER

WALKER

SCOTSWOOD

WESTMORLAND ROAD

RIVER TYNE

CENTRAL STATION

GATESHEAD & DISTRICT

Map of the Newcastle network as at 1945.

Newcastle Corporation No 285 pictured at the entrance to Gosforth Park taken after the war, but before the trolleybus overhead was erected in late 1946 to 1947. The track continued and went through the gates that can just be seen to the other side at West Moor. The line passed alongside the Race Course Grandstand where there was a four-track station. From the opening of the Gosforth Park Light Railway in 1923/24, there was a regular circular service through the park in spring, summer and autumn using open-top bogie cars. F. N. T. Lloyd-Jones/Online Transport Archive

United Automobile, and in furtherance of this, two batches of trolleybuses were ordered during 1946: thirty-six in February and fifty in November. The former were budgeted to cost £3,786 each, but the corporation was warned that delivery would be delayed and the vehicles were not in fact received until early 1949. The total cost of the fifty trolleybuses ordered in November was almost £260,000 with the order being split between BUT and Sunbeam for the chassis, and Metro-Cammell and Northern Coachbuilders for the bodies. The 1946 Act included powers to abandon the Gosforth Park Light Railway and permit the construction of a road to take the replacement trolleybuses. The 1946 Act authorised the expenditure of £40,000 on road work, £215,000 on electrical installations and £570,000 on new vehicles.

That the conversion of the tramway system to trolleybus operation remained the corporation's policy was confirmed in late 1945 and reflected in the contemporary press. *Commercial Motor* covered the story in its issue of 7 December with the headline 'Trolleybuses to replace Newcastle's Trams', with the story noting that as 'soon as opportunity occurs, the Corporation of Newcastle-upon-Tyne has decided that its trams shall be displaced by trolleybuses,' quoting the general manager Henry Citford Godsmark on the difficulties of operating services at a time of shortages of labour and materials.

The first post-war conversion occurred on 1 June 1946 when the largely single-track route west of Scotswood to Throckley was converted to bus operation; 'B' class No 253 was the last tram at Throckley; the service from the centre to Scotswood continued until October 1948 with a peak-hours service operating until 11 September 1949. This withdrawal was, however, partially offset by the reintroduction of tram services over the Gosforth Park Light Railway for the first time since spring

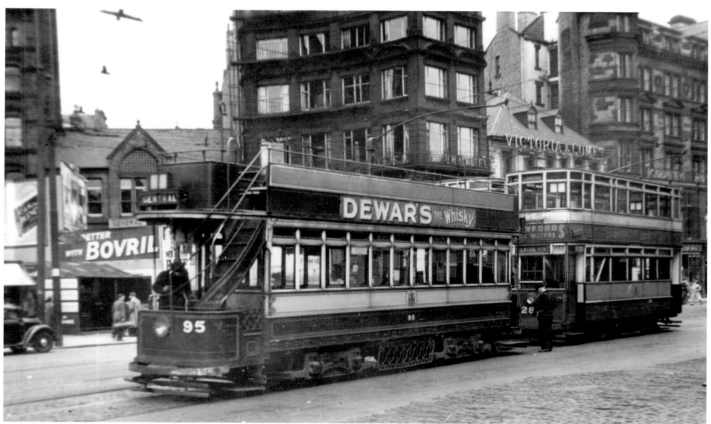

1940. Services over the line had been suspended just before the fall of France in 1940, although the track was retained and used for storing and scrapping withdrawn trams. Special services reappeared in July 1946 in connection with greyhound and horse racing in the park. The introduction of the special services was, however, overshadowed by a fatal accident on 8 July 1946 when No 276 derailed and collided with No 300; one person was killed and several injured. The corporation had acquired the track in the park at scrap value following the conversion of the Tyneside Tramways & Tramroads Co system in 1930, but had invested little in it thereafter.

In 1946 Godsmark died at the early age of fifty; he was replaced as general manager by Frank S. Taylor. Summer 1946 witnessed progress on the proposed conversion of the Gosforth route to trolleybus operation. However,

as Gateshead & District retained running powers, provision needed to be maintained for tram operation. Discussions were ongoing between the corporations of Gateshead and Newcastle over future transport policy, two – on 7 August and 3 October – being held in 1946. At the latter meeting it was noted that the police would not permit trolleybuses wider than 7ft 6in to operate over the High Level Bridge.

Other work continued towards the implementation of the conversion programme. In May 1946 the construction of a new substation at Cartington Terrace, North Heaton, was approved, and six months later an upgrade to the existing substation at West Moor was also sanctioned. In December 1946 an agreement between Gateshead & District and Newcastle Corporation for the through running of trolleybuses was made and in early 1947 Newcastle Corporation

A busy scene in front of Newcastle Central station sees open-top Class F No 95 awaiting its next duties. Newcastle was the last major urban operator in Britain to use open-top cars in regular passenger service, with the last not being withdrawn until 1949. C. Carter

Gone are the glory days for the Gosforth Park Light Railway; long used to carrying large numbers of race-goers to sporting events, once the post-war conversion programme resumed, the rusting tracks within the park were used to store withdrawn trams awaiting their fate. Here, closest to the camera, is No 115, one of the six Class A cars that survived the war. No 115 was withdrawn in 1947.
F. N. T. Lloyd-Jones/Online Transport Archive

ordered 517 traction columns, 100 bracket arms and 22 miles of overhead wire. In February 1947 approval was given for the purchase of the land for the construction of a turning circle at Gosforth Park. However, work on conversion was slower than anticipated and, as a result, much-needed attention was given to the condition of the track on the remaining routes, and a number of the single-deck cars used on the Benton route were overhauled. In addition, No 282, due to be scrapped following an accident, was repaired and restored to service. The delays to the conversion programme led the *Newcastle Chronicle* to argue for 'leaving the trams for the time being to carry the big traffic which goes to Benton and High Heaton' in late 1947, but time was running out for Newcastle's trams.

By February the first of the corporation's new BUT trolleybuses were being delivered, although these were stored at Byker following delivery until the conversion of the Gosforth Park route. By 31 March 1948 the trolleybus overhead was largely complete and, on 16 April,

the Gosforth Park route was converted to trolleybus operation with No 290 being the last car to Gosforth Park. Thereafter, Gateshead's trams on the Low Fell to Gosforth Park route terminated at Central station. The trolleybuses terminated at the south end of the Gosforth Park Light Railway; in the end, the section from the West Gates via West Moor over the light railway to Benton was never converted to trolleybus operation. With work completed on the Gosforth Park route, the overhead gang turned its attention to erecting trolleybus overhead on the Benton and West Jesmond routes. Following the conversion, forty-six cars – mostly older types but including a handful of the more modern ones such as No 191 – were scrapped at a siding at West Moor; some had been stored for twelve months but others were more recent casualties.

The Gosforth Park conversion saw other service alterations in April 1948. Saltwell Park cars now terminated at Monument, and the Heworth-Chillingham circle was split with cars, for the former now terminated at Haymarket and corporation cars from Chillingham or Shieldhall at Pilgrim Street. Despite its scheduled conversion, the route to West Jesmond saw, during the summer of 1948, a certain amount of track work undertaken. June 1948 saw work completed, at a cost of £15,000, on improving the clearance at the West Street railway bridge in Gateshead; although the new height was sufficient for double-deck buses or trolleybuses, it was still inadequate to permit the operation of double-deck trams.

On 31 October 1948 the bulk of the remaining tram routes in Newcastle were converted; the routes affected were those to West Moor and Forest Hall as well as the service from New Bridge Street to Chillingham that had only been introduced on 18 April 1948. By January 1949 only one dedicated Newcastle route remained operational – that to Scotswood with its peak hours extension to Byker – although corporation trams continued to serve the joint routes to Gateshead from their terminus at Central station, for which twenty cars were required. The track and overhead to West Moor was retained for about telve months to permit the movement of cars for scrap to the siding there; once this ceased, the final cars were destined to be scrapped at Byker Depot. The Scotswood service with its

Newcastle Corporation No 219, one of the Brush-built balcony cars of 1914, stands at the Wrekenton terminus on 26 February 1950. By this stage, Newcastle's trams had less than a week to go before final withdrawal. Tony Wickens/Online Transport Archive (262)

Byker extension ceased to operate on 10 September 1949.

The end of Newcastle's trams came on 4 March 1950 when the surviving cars were withdrawn from the joint services

Newcastle No 289 is pictured on the long section of single track with passing loops between Sheriff Hill and Wrekenton on 4 March 1950 – the last day of tramway operation by the corporation. John Meredith/Online Transport Archive (102/1)

from Central station to Saltwell Park and Wrekenton. The services continued to operate using trams from Gateshead & District until the following year; with the decision of Gateshead & District not to exercise its trolleybus powers but to seek tramway replacement by buses, once the final withdrawal occurred in August 1951, it was the diesel bus that dominated. Such was the low-key nature of Newcastle's final demise that the number of the last car to operate was not recorded.

Newcastle Depots

Newcastle entered the Second World War with three operational tram depots, although one, Wingrove Road (closed 3 June 1944), did not survive the war. Of the city's other two surviving tram depots, Haymarket (located on Haymarket towards the north of the city centre, but actually served by lines off Northumberland Street) was closed to trams on 17 April 1948. The last tram depot, and location of the corporation's

main workshops, was at Byker on Shields Road, which closed on 4 March 1950. The city's surviving trams were scrapped at Byker following closure of the system.

Newcastle Closures

1 June 1946
Throckley-Scotswood Bridge

16 April 1948
Gosforth

31 October 1948
Forest Hall; West Moor; Chillingham/ Shieldfield

10 September 1949
Scotswood Bridge

4 March 1950
Saltwell Park; Wrekenton

Newcastle Fleet

1-28, 192

These twenty-nine cars represented Class H. They were four-wheel double-deck cars built to replace the earlier single-

Newcastle No 10 was one of the 29-strong 'H' class of balcony-top four-wheel cars supplied between 1906 and 1910. All survived the war, but withdrawals commenced in 1946.
Burrow Bros via Online Transport Archive

deck cars that had been delivered for the start of the system. Constructed with corporation-built open-balcony bodies on Brill 21E trucks, the trams were delivered between 1906 and 1910. Following the withdrawal of a number of the class in 1946, the following 1, 3, 13/17, 22/24/26 were renumbered 24/26, 17/13, 1, 22 and 3 respectively. In 1947 No 120 was also renumbered 24; No 120 had been offered for sale but its condition was better than No 24 so the two cars swapped identity. All were withdrawn during the period from 1946 to 1949.

29, 42/43, 52/54, 77, 80/88

In 1902 a batch of sixty cars, Nos 29-88, were supplied with Hurst Nelson single-deck bodies on Brill 27G bogies.

The Class C cars originally had open compartments at both vestibule ends, but most were rebuilt as fully enclosed during the period from the First World War through to 1927. During 1921/22 ten cars – Nos 32/34, 45/48, 59, 61/69, 73, 76 and 78 – were rebuilt as open-balcony double-deckers. In 1923, to operate the through services to Gateshead, Nos 29, 31/36/38-40/42/43/47/49, 52-55/57/58, 60/63/67, 70/72/77, 80/86/88 received replacement Peckham P25 bogies. Nos 29, 42/43, 52/54, 77, 80 and 88 were also rebodied during 1932 and 1933. Apart from the rebodied eight trams, the remainder of the type were scrapped before 1940. Of the survivors, all were withdrawn in 1948 and sold: Nos 29, 42 and 77 went to Grimsby &

Newcastle No 43 was one of eight survivors into 1945 of a batch of sixty cars originally delivered in 1901. All eight, known as 'Pullmans', had undergone significant modernisation during their careers and all were sold for further service following withdrawal in Newcastle. No 43 did not travel far as it was one of five sold to neighbouring Gateshead.
F. N. T. Lloyd-Jones/Online Transport Archive

Only a handful of British tram operators possessed open-top trams in the post-war years; of these, only one was in north-east England, Newcastle. One of the type, No 104, shows the open-top body with which most of the class were fitted only a couple of years after delivery as single-deck cars. Rebuilt, the trams could seat thirty-six on the lower deck and forty-eight on the upper. Similar car No 102 now forms part of the National Tramway Museum collection.
F. N. T. Lloyd-Jones/Online Transport Archive

Immingham (as Nos 6-8), and Nos 43, 52/54, 80/88 went to Gateshead (as Nos 74/76/73/75/77 respectively).

89-97/99-110

Nos 89-110 represented the Class F bogie double-deck cars that were built in 1903 as rebuilds of single-deck semi-convertible trams supplied by Hurst Nelson in 1901. Originally open-top and unvestibuled, the twenty-two cars were built with bodies supplied by the corporation on Brill 27G bogies. Between 1905 and 1907, Nos 96, 105/08 were rebuilt with open-balcony top covers; from No 105 these were removed shortly after the end of the First World War. Nos 96 and 108 subsequently received enclosed vestibules. Nos 90/92, 100/07/09 were rebuilt, the first during the First World War, with open-balcony tops and enclosed vestibules. No 89 was rebuilt with a fully enclosed top-deck during the same programme, but did not receive an enclosed vestibule until 1926. No 98 was

destroyed by fire in 1917; withdrawal of the other wenty-one cars took place between 1946 and 1949. No 102 was preserved after closure and is now part of the National Tramway Museum collection.

111/15/20/21/27/30

These six cars represented the survivors of the twenty-strong Class A, which were built with open-top unvestibuled bodies supplied by Hurst Nelson on Brill 21E trucks in 1901. Open-balcony tops were fitted between 1905 and 1907. The six cars that remained in service after the war had all received enclosed vestibules in 1933 with the remainder of the class sold to Sheffield in 1941. All bar No 120, renumbered 24, were withdrawn in 1947. The lower deck of No 114, withdrawn as Sheffield No 317 in 1951, was secured from a farm near Scunthorpe for preservation. Reaching Beamish in 1987, it has been fully restored to original Newcastle open-top condition.

No 120 was one of the six surviving Class A that remained with Newcastle Corporation following the sale of the other fourteen members of the class to Sheffield Corporation in 1941. The six survivors had all been fitted with enclosed vestibules in 1933. It is seen here towards the end of its life in a somewhat battered condition. R. R. Clark

170-91

Originally delivered as open-top unvestibuled four-wheel trams during 1903 and 1904, these twenty-two cars were Class G and were fitted with corporation-built bodies on Brill 21E trucks. All were rebuilt as fully enclosed between 1927 and 1929. All were withdrawn from service by the end of 1949.

Seen alongside 'B' class No 257, Newcastle No 189 was one of 22 'G' class cars delivered originally during 1903 and 1904. Rebuilt in the late 1920s, all were withdrawn from service by the end of 1949. J. Joyce Collection/Online Transport Archive

The first of the third batch of Class E double-deck cars, No 225, which was delivered in 1915, is seen outside Newcastle Central station on 4 March 1950. The tram's very poor external condition emphasises the fact that this was the last day of service for corporation trams and No 225 would shortly make its final one-way journey to the scrapyard.
John Meredith/Online Transport Archive (100/9)

193-229

These were the Class E four-wheel double-deckers. Nos 193-209 had Newcastle-built bodies and were delivered between 1912 and 1914. Nos 210-24 were built by Brush in 1914, and Nos 225-29 were fitted with corporation-built bodies and delivered between 1915 and 1918. All were fitted with Brill 21E trucks with the exception of Nos 203/04/06/07/10/11/15/16, which received Peckham P22 trucks. All had open-balcony top covers but lower-deck vestibules. All were withdrawn between 1947 and 1950.

232-36/40-50/52-309

The Class B fully enclosed double-deckers were delivered between 1917 and 1920 (Nos 232-36), and between 1921 and 1926 (Nos 240-309). The first batch had bodies supplied from the corporation's own workshops, and the later cars were all bodied by Brush. All were fitted with Peckham P22 trucks, although No 232 received a Brill 21E by 1940. In 1924 No 269 became a six-wheel car – with a four-wheel truck and additional single axle – followed by No 309 two years later; No 269 was converted in 1927 to operate on two maximum-traction trucks. Nos 269 and 309 were subsequently reconverted to conventional four-wheel cars. The only casualty before 1946 – when Nos 276 and 300 were withdrawn following a collision

The highest-numbered Newcastle tram, and last new tram top to be delivered, was Class B No 309, which entered service in 1926. Built originally by Brush, the car is seen at Museum on 4 March 1950, its last day of service.
John Meredith/Online Transport Archive (101/7)

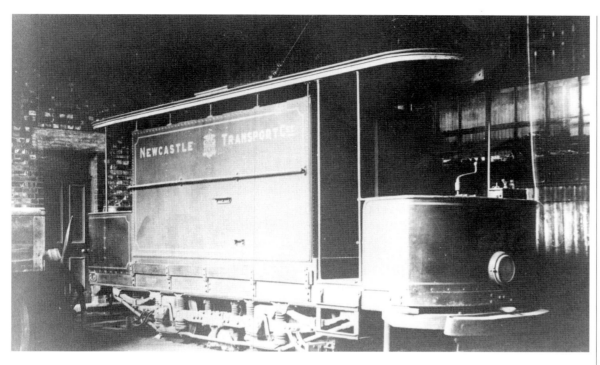

Newcastle No 237 was a purpose-built railgrinder built by the corporation in 1921. It was withdrawn in 1947, but had been out of use for some time before its official demise.
Barry Cross Collection/ Online Transport Archive

that resulted in one death and 30 injured – was No 251 that was withdrawn in 1924 following an accident. All the survivors were withdrawn between 1947 and 1950.

237

Built in Newcastle's own workshops in 1921 on a Peckham P22 four-wheel truck, No 237 was a purpose-built rail grinder. It was withdrawn finally in 1947, although had been out of use for some time before withdrawal.

310-12

These three cars were sand and salt cars and were converted by the corporation between 1921 and 1923 utilising parts from scrapped older trams. All three were fitted with Brill 21E four-wheel trucks and were withdrawn by 1949.

Two of Newcastle's sand and salt cars, Nos 310 and 311, are pictured at the depot at Byker. These two, plus No 312, were built by the corporation in the early 1920s and survived until 1949.
F. N. T. Lloyd-Jones/Online Transport Archive

ROTHERHAM

The survival of the tramway system in Rotherham until as late as 1949 is down to one fact: the town's proximity to Sheffield. The town had been a pioneer of trolleybus operation and, with the exception of the through route to Sheffield via Templeborough – for which English Electric had supplied eleven single-ended streamlined cars in the mid-1930s – all the town's tram routes had been converted before the Second World War. In the immediate post-war years Sheffield remained wedded to the tram and so, consequently, did Rotherham for the one route. However, the necessity of replacing the A630 road bridge

over the railway at Tinsley caused the withdrawal – temporarily in theory – of the through service on 12 December 1948, resulting in the Rotherham cars operating a shuttle between the town centre and Templeborough as the crossover at Tinsley was unsuitable for the single-ended cars.

The sentiments of the Rotherham side can be gauged by the comments of the general manager as reported in *Modern Tramway* at the time: 'We are hoping that tramcars will never again run between Rotherham and Sheffield, as the cost of replacing the tram track over the bridge will be very high. My committee

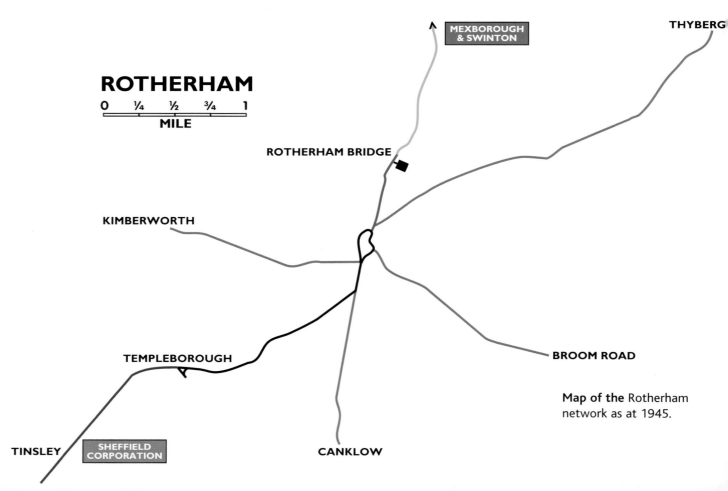

ROTHERHAM

0   ¼   ½   ¾   1
MILE

MEXBOROUGH & SWINTON

THYBERG

ROTHERHAM BRIDGE

KIMBERWORTH

BROOM ROAD

TEMPLEBOROUGH

Map of the Rotherham network as at 1945.

TINSLEY

SHEFFIELD CORPORATION

CANKLOW

are very anxious that tramcars shall be discontinued, but it is not yet certain that the Sheffield Transport Committee are of the same opinion. Personally, I think this will mean the end of the through tram service to Sheffield and if this position arises it is our intention to do away with all our trams on the Rotherham-Sheffield route between Rotherham and the borough boundary.'

The general manager got his way; the through tram service was never reinstated and the final Rotherham trams operated on 12 November 1949. The last car to operate was one of the English Electric streamlined cars, No 11.

Rotherham Depot

Rotherham possessed a single tram depot – Rawmarsh Road – that was sited virtually at the terminus of the Canklow

route and required the retention of the bulk of this largely single-track with passing loops line following its closure on 9 July 1934. The depot closed as a tram depot with the abandonment of the system on 13 November 1949.

Rotherham Closure

13 November 1949
Rotherham-Templeborough

Rotherham Fleet

1-11

To operate the through service to Sheffield, Rotherham acquired two batches of single-ended trams in 1934 (Nos 1-6) and 1935 (Nos 7-11). These were constructed with English Electric bodies on EMB Hornless four-wheel trucks. All survived in service until the withdrawal

With the local branch of Marks & Spencer, closed in 2004 when the store relocated, in the background, Rotherham single-ended car No 11 turns right from College Street on the single-track town centre loop in Rotherham before heading towards Templeborough.
F. N. T. Lloyd-Jones/Online Transport Archive

One of the eleven single-ended trams that Rotherham acquired in the mid-1930s to operate the through service to Sheffield, No 7, is seen with a Sheffield tram. Both vehicles operated in blue and cream livery.
Unknown photographer/ Online Transport Archive

The only post-war survivor of Rotherham's fleet before the delivery of the single-ended cars in the mid-1930s was No 12. Originally delivered in 1902 as one of the first trams delivered to the corporation, No 12 was fully enclosed as late as 1942.
J. H. Roberts/Online Transport Archive

of the Rotherham-Templeborough service in November 1949. All were scrapped following withdrawal.

12

Although the bulk of Rotherham's older tramcars were withdrawn in the mid-1930s with the arrival of the single-ended cars, No 12 survived. It was one of the original batch of twelve cars – Nos 1-12 – delivered in 1902, but was not the original No 12 and its original fleet number is uncertain. The car was originally an open-top four-wheeler with a body supplied by ER&TCW on a Brill 21E truck. A number of the batch were rebuilt with domed-top roofs between 1906 and 1913, and it was one of these

modified cars that survived. It was rebuilt as fully enclosed in 1942 and was scrapped after withdrawal in 1949.

14

In 1942, to supplement the fleet during the war when it was suffering vehicle shortages, Rotherham hired Leeds Corporation No 125A. This dated originally to 1908 and had a Kirkstall Works-built body on a Brill 21E truck. Originally No 125, it became 125A in 1925 and was renumbered 14 on arrival in Rotherham. Rotherham converted the vehicle from open-balcony to fully enclosed and purchased the car outright in 1948. It survived until 1949 and was scrapped on withdrawal.

The two non-single-ended cars that Rotherham possessed post-war are both seen, along with a single-deck trolleybus, outside the depot at Rotherham Bridge. No 14, nearest to the camera, had originally been hired from Leeds Corporation in 1942, but was purchased by Rotherham six years later. Richard Wiseman

SHEFFIELD

At the end of the war Sheffield, although lacking the reserved track sections that were a feature of other progressive tramways, was regarded as one of the most secure tramways in Britain. Traditional in operation – its entire fleet until closure were four-wheel cars provided with conventional trolley poles – Sheffield's trams were popular with passengers but,

ultimately, fell foul of a Labour Party that dominated local politics.

In the interwar years, there had been three short abandonments: Petre Street on 19 April 1925, Nether Edge on 24 March 1934 and Fulwood via Broomhill on 22 August 1936. However, these had been countered by extensions elsewhere, culminating in two extensions to the Fulwood route in 1935 that opened on

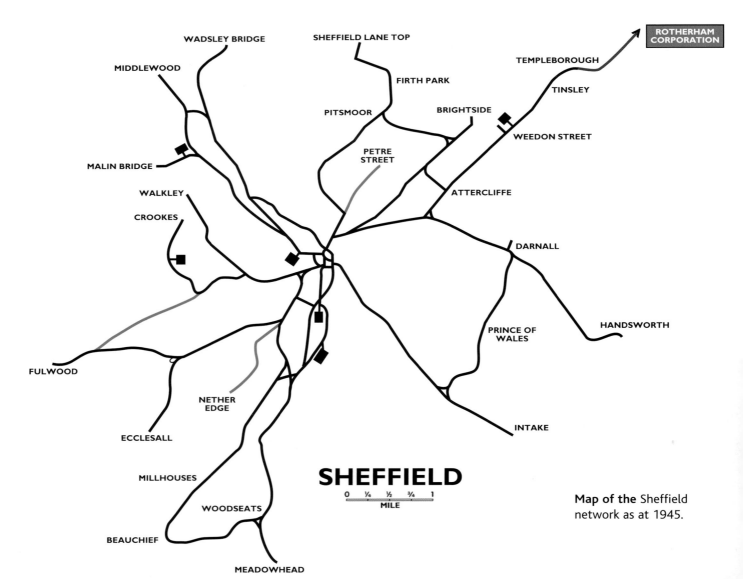

SHEFFIELD

0 ¼ ½ ¾ 1
MILE

Map of the Sheffield network as at 1945.

Pictured at Meadowhead on 28 August 1949, Sheffield No 275 was one of fifty cars delivered between 1936 and 1939. Sheffield was the last British tramway operated exclusively by four-wheel trams.
John Meredith/Online Transport Archive (83/2)

8 February and 29 December. Further planned extensions were, however, put on hold at the start of the Second World War and never resurrected. At the start of the war, Sheffield had a fleet of 443 passenger cars; despite the wartime losses, the result of the construction of the replacement cars, plus the acquisition of second-hand trams from Bradford and Newcastle, saw the fleet increased to 468 in 1945.

The Sheffield livery of the late 1940s came in two styles: the simplified version as exemplified by No 275 in the previous photograph and the pre-war blue with ornate lining out as shown here by No 102 at Sheffield Lane Top on 28 August 1949.
John Meredith/Online Transport Archive (83/3)

The immediate post-war period started with an air of optimism. A new manager – R. C. Moore who had been appointed deputy general manager in 1945 – was made general manager following the retirement of Harris Watson. In the following year the corporation marked the fiftieth anniversary of municipal tram operation. One of the ex-horse cars converted for works use, No 375, was restored to its original condition as No 15 and was used in public service for a week during July 1946 between Leopold Street and The Moor. More significantly, perhaps, the first new tram to be built since the war, No 501, was officially launched on 12 August 1946. Although not known at the time, No 501 was destined to be the last tram constructed at Queen's Road Works. Another positive note was struck in early 1948 for the department to borrow £200,000 to fund the purchase of thirty-five new cars at an estimated price of £6,850 each, and tenders were also sought for the supply of new manganese steel track and crossings.

The first threat to the tramway system came towards the end of the decade with problems with the through service to Rotherham. Rotherham had struggled to provide enough cars to serve the route – indeed had borrowed from Sheffield two cars at a time for up to five days at a stretch during the first four months of 1947 (a total of fifty cars being loaned during the period) – and the single-ended cars were demonstrating their poor overall condition. The need to replace the railway bridge at Tinsley resulted in the through service being initially suspended on 12 December 1948 and then, following agreement, withdrawn the following year. The suspension meant that Sheffield's trams ceased to operate over the Vulcan Road to Templeborough section.

Following the closure of the through service, twenty-five trams were withdrawn by 31 March 1950. These included a

The bulk of the Sheffield system was traditional street tramway, but there were odd sections of reserved track, most notably along Prince of Wales Road. No 70 heads along this stretch of track on 28 August 1949. The absence of other road traffic is notable.
John Meredith/Online Transport Archive (83/4)

number of the ex-Newcastle Cars (Nos 312/14/16/17/20-24) and ex-Bradford cars (Nos 326-29/32) as well as a number of the Brush-built cars of 1924/25 (Nos 36/37 and 46), two of the surviving UEC cars of 1907 (Nos 336 and 345), four of the Brush-built cars of 1919-22 (Nos 414/19/25/27) and two of the Cravens-built cars of 1926/27 (Nos 468/93). Of these, Nos 345, 419 and 493 were withdrawn as a result of accident damage (No 345 had been in store since 1947). These withdrawals included the first trams built after the First World War to succumb. Another tram withdrawn due to an accident was No 438, which was involved in a collision on 17 July 1950 when a lorry ran into it on Derbyshire Lane, injuring eighteen passengers.

The first of the thirty-five new trams ordered from Charles H. Roberts of Horbury, No 502, entered service on 15 May 1950. By the end of the year Nos 502-10 had been delivered and in service; initially the new cars operated on the Middlewood-Ecclesall, Intake-Walkley and Prince of Wales Road routes. Alongside the construction of new cars, the corporation also overhauled

or rebuilt a significant number of trams from 1948 onwards. Between 1948 and 1950, 20 cars had body overhauls, 15 of which were classified as major (Nos 61, 71/76, 131/ 34/35/43/45/55, 218, 416/36/41/47/97) and five minor (Nos 109, 278, 367, 413/69). Of these, five cars – Nos 367, 413/41/47/69 – were also fitted with smaller handbrakes that resulted in the replacement of their banjo-shaped windscreens.

The delivery of the new cars resulted in the withdrawal of a number of older trams. On 1 July 1951, Nos 9, 22, 80/88, 90-93, 101/06/20/37-9/42, 432/39/ 43/44/59/6196 were taken out of service; these were followed by Nos 347 (22 July 1952), 348 (26 October 1951) and 350 (19 March 1953).

The critical event in the history of Sheffield trams post-war occurred on 4 April 1951 when a report advocating the replacement of the tramway system by bus was presented. The vote went along party lines: the Conservatives and the Liberals voted to retain the trams, but the dominant Labour group voted to accept the plan. The only exception was Councillor R. W. Allott who resigned

The tram service between Fulwood and Malin Bridge was converted, despite much opposition, to bus operation on 5 January 1952. 'Standard' No 189, which was later preserved, stands at the Fulwood terminus. R. W. A. Jones/Online Transport Archive (SD1)

No 35 was one of eleven cars repainted in an all-over one-tone green livery between March and July 1952. A further twelve cars appeared in a two-tone version. The new livery was not favourably received and all twenty-three had reverted to traditional blue and cream by the end of the following year. Marcus Eavis/Online Transport Archive

from the Labour Party as a result. Such a proposal was, however, not going to be accepted by the electorate automatically and the Sheffield Tramways Development Association was formed to fight the plans. Petitions were organised, particularly after the first proposed abandonments were announced on 24 December 1951; these demonstrated great opposition to the proposed conversion.

The first abandonment took place, despite the opposition, on 5 January 1952 with the Fulwood-Malin Bridge route; the last car from Fulwood to Malin Bridge was No 65. No trams were withdrawn as a consequence of this conversion. The revised bus services found little favour and there were demands for the trams to be reinstated. Councillor Siddall, a noted opponent of the abandonment policy, commented: 'We deplore the fact that Sheffield people should be put to an enormous amount of inconvenience and

that an efficient transport system should be abandoned in favour of a fixed idea.' A proposal to the council on 5 March 1952 that the trams be reinstated was, however, rejected.

Although closure was now the avowed policy of the corporation, work continued on overhauling the existing tram fleet and the delivery of the new Roberts-built cars continued. In April 1954 both ends of No 55 were rebuilt, and between 1951 and 1954 six cars had major overhauls: three were classified as major (Nos 121, 203 and 209 – the last following accident damage at Meadowhead) and three minor (Nos 123/50 and 219). In addition, between 1952 and 1956 twenty-three cars received rebuilt lower-deck saloons: Nos 25/27, 68/69, 72/73/75, 87/89, 97/98, 102/15/ 22/28/51/61/67/70/73/74/83/91. The last of these treated, No 183, received attention in 1956 as the result of accident damage and was probably the last car repainted from the old to new livery. Between 1954 and 1956 a further six cars received major overhauls: Nos 62, 74/77, 148/53/54.

If the closure policy was heavily opposed, another innovation that occurred in 1952 was also widely deprecated. Between March and July 1952 twenty-three cars emerged in experimental green liveries: Nos 33, 76, 150, 211-13/15/19/53/64/84/90 in two-tone green with Nos 32/35, 73, 202/16/ 21/52/56/85-87 in one-tone. The first to appear was No 150 with No 221 the last to emerge. The negative reaction led to the decision to abandon the experiment and all twenty-three reverted to traditional blue by December 1953.

With the conversion policy now in place, the Sheffield Tramways Development Association sent a petition with almost 8,000 names to the Ministry of Transport demanding that the policy be reversed. The Ministry responded, according to the *Sheffield Telegraph*, by pointing out to the council the need for austerity in capital investment and that conversion could not be justified in the national interest. The council noted these comments, but only deferred the policy

The Ecclesall to Middlewood route was converted to bus operation on 27 March 1954 – the only route to succumb between January 1952 and April 1956. 'Roberts' No 515, then relatively new, is pictured at Ecclesall awaiting departure with a service to Middlewood. R. W. A. Jones/Online Transport Archive (SD15)

rather than abandoning it.

Early 1952 witnessed the decision to allow external advertising on trams for the first time in thirty-six years along

The terminus at Middlewood with No 280, delivered just before the Second World War, closest to the camera. The service between Middlewood and Ecclesall was converted to bus operation on 27 March 1954. R. W. A. Jones/Online Transport Archive (SD30)

with the entry into service of the last of the Roberts-built cars, No 536, on 11 April. However, the tramway conversion programme was confirmed in early 1953 when the Transport Committee agreed that the next stage would see the conversion of the Middlewood-Ecclesall service. In addition, the purchase of 56 new buses for £224,624 was approved. The conversion of the route took place on 27 March 1954, slightly earlier than proposed and despite the presentation of a petition by the STDA that contained more than 11,000 names objecting to the conversion. It also saw the withdrawal of twenty-eight Brush- and Cravens-built cars and the closure, following the removal of the last cars on 23 April, of

the depot at Holme Lane. The last car at Ecclesall was No 234 and at Middlewood No 513. The 28 cars withdrawn were despatched to Thos W. Ward at Tinsley, entering the scrapyard via a siding built in 1951 to permit the movement of withdrawn cars direct to the yard. The result of the withdrawals meant that, by 31 March 1954, the tram fleet had been reduced to 369.

In late 1953 work commenced on the widening of the canal bridge on Staniforth Road, which was completed in early 1954. While the work was in hand, the only traffic permitted to use the bridge was trams and these used an unpaved single track laid to one side of the bridge. In 1956 the track across the bridge was modified with conventional double track in place of the interlaced track used previously; it was believed that this was

'Standard' No 190 emerges from Angel Street with a service to Millhouses; the line through Angel Street was singled in July 1955.
Phil Tatt/Online Transport Archive (1407)

Another of the batch of cars delivered between 1936 and 1939, No 300, stands at the Intake terminus; following a two-year period, conversion of the Sheffield system recommenced in the summer of 1956. On 6 October 1956 the section of line between Elm Tree and Intake was converted to bus operation. Adverts only began to appear on the exterior of trams in the early 1950s.
Phil Tatt/Online Transport Archive

the last piece of interlaced track in use on a British tramway. Reflecting the fact that, in theory, the tramways still had a decade of life, it was agreed in early 1954 to borrow £100,000 to fund track work on the routes that were deemed those to survive the longest. During 1955 a certain amount of track work was undertaken. This included the singling, between 15 and 18 July, of the track in Angel Street. This was used primarily for access downhill to Tenter Street Depot, although the line was still wired for bi-directional running. Also undertaken in 1955 was the removal of the direct line from Tinsley Depot to Weedon Street.

Although no routes were converted between March 1954 and April 1956, the fleet continued to contract. Some twelve cars (Nos 58-60, 132/36, 344/87, 400/70/73/86/90) were withdrawn during the year ended 31 March 1955 and nineteen (Nos 53, 343/46/77/78/83/94, 433/36/63/67/69/74/75/88/89/94/95/99) by 31 March 1956. This meant that the passenger fleet now totalled 338 cars.

The service from Crookes to Handsworth was converted to bus operation on 4 May 1957; here 'Roberts' No 529 is pictured having just arrived at the Crookes terminus and about to head back towards Handsworth. The abandonment of this route resulted in the closure of the depot at Crookes.
R. W. A. Jones/Online Transport Archive (SD52)

The next conversion, for which it was estimated that forty-five buses would be required, was the Walkley-Intake route. This was completed on 7 April 1956 and also included the supplementary route from Midland Station and Fitzalan Square to Walkley as well as the City Road portion of the Prince of Wales Road circle. No 55 was the last car at Walkley and No 505 at Intake via City Road; the last cars to traverse the Prince of Wales Road circle were Nos 65 and 94. Thereafter, most cars using the Prince of Wales Road terminated at Intake (Elm Tree). These conversions permitted the withdrawal of forty trams, all of which were sold to Thos W. Ward. These withdrawals meant that the number of rocker panel cars in service was reduced to four: Nos 42, 52, 456/97. The

first Sheffield tram preserved officially, No 342, was acquired at this stage by the British Transport Commission.

In late summer 1956 licences were applied for to undertake the conversion of the Vulcan Road, and Intake-Brightside via Prince of Wales Road and Darnall routes. The conversion was undertaken on 6 October 1956, although the only section to see all trams withdrawn was that between Intake (Elm Tree) and Intake (Birley Vale). No 176 was the last car that operated from Intake to Tinsley, and No 117 was the last car from Intake, with a service for the city centre via Prince of Wales Road. The conversions during 1956 resulted in the fleet being reduced to 265 passenger cars by 31 March 1957.

The next route to succumb was that

from Crookes to Handsworth on 4 May 1957. This stage also included the peak-hours services from Crookes and Handsworth to Brightside and Vulcan Road. The last car at Crookes, at 1.30 am on 5 May, was No 194, and the last car to depart from Handsworth was No 33. Also closed at this time was the depot at Crookes. One of the casualties at this time was No 141, which was the first car in the more modern livery to be withdrawn. On 23 June 1957 there were some minor alterations to service times. The last trams were altered to run at 11.15 pm rather than 11.30 pm – a change originally introduced as a consequence of the fuel crisis post-Suez – and the outward night trams were altered from midnight and 12.30 am to 11.45 pm and 12.15 am respectively. The inbound night trams remained unchanged at 12.50 am and 1.30 am. It was also noted at this time

that Nos 164/69/88/89/94/96 had been repainted from the old to new livery; it was believed at the time that these would be the last cars to be so treated.

In August 1957 Nos 133 and 263 were withdrawn following a collision; the fact they were not repaired indicated the trams were now living on borrowed time. On 26 October 1957 the service from Exchange Street to Sheffield Lane Top was converted to bus operation; this permitted the removal of trams from the loop along Exchange Street for redevelopment. An increased frequency of other services to Sheffield Lane Top compensated for this withdrawal. On 4 January 1958 the track between Midland Station and the Moor, via Furnival Street, was abandoned except for a terminal stub at the Moor end; this was probably one of the last sections of single track with passing loops used by any British

One of the batch of 25 cars built by W. & E. Hill Ltd of South Shields, No 143, is seen at the terminus at Handsworth. This service was converted to bus operation on 4 May 1957.
R. W. A. Jones/Online Transport Archive (SD13)

The Intake (Elm Tree) to Fitzalan Square, via Prince of Wales Road, was converted to bus operation on 12 April 1958. No 122, one of seventy cars built by the corporation between 1930 and 1933, and one of the thirteen of the type that received a rebuilt lower deck in the early 1950s, is pictured on Prince of Wales Road.
Phil Tatt/Online Transport Archive (1433)

tramway. The last cars to use the through line were Nos 219/49. The surviving terminal stubs came into their own on 17 May 1958 when there was a royal visit by the Queen Mother; services were suspended in part of the city centre and cars terminated using the Furnival Street stub.

Between 1 January 1958 and the next conversion, on 12 April 1958, thirteen trams were withdrawn – Nos 155-58/66/87/90/93/96/98, 209/14/29 – which left only eighteen cars still in the old livery. The next casualty was the route from Intake (Elm Tree) to Fitzalan Square via Prince of Wales Road, which was converted to bus operation on 12

April 1958. The last car at Intake (Elm Tree) was No 300, and the last car to use the Darnall Road siding was No 210. The conversion resulted in the withdrawal of 31 cars, of which 12 were in the old livery – Nos 71, 126/62/64/68/69/71/72/88/89/94/95 – of which No 189 was retained as it was destined for preservation. A total of 19 cars in the new livery – Nos 61, 74, 109/29/31/34/35/43/59, 202/07/13/17/39/41/45/46/55/76 – also succumbed at this stage.

On 5 October 1958 a new roundabout was brought into use at the junction of the Moor with Ecclesall Road that resulted in 100yd of reserved track to the system as the trams passed through the centre of the roundabout. By this date the tram fleet had been reduced to 169 passenger cars, of which only six – Nos 63, 160/63/65/97/99 – were in the old-style livery. The final conversion of 1958 occurred on 6 December with the replacement of the Fitzalan Square to Brightside service by buses; this conversion also affected the factory-hours service from Brightside via Upwell Street and Firth Park to Sheffield Lane Top. The part-day service between Fitzalan Square and Sheffield Lane Top remained operational, and so the only track abandoned at this stage was the outer section of the route to Brightside beyond Upwell Street. The last car to Brightside was No 210, and the last car from Brightside to Sheffield Lane Top was No 191.

Although the story of trams in Sheffield during 1959 and 1960 is one of continued contraction and closure, there were odd moments of levity. One of these occurred on 27 January 1959 when an escaped parrot caused a temporary cessation of services as a result of perching on the overhead. The next conversions – Fitzalan Square to Sheffield Lane Top via Savile Street and Woodseats (Camping Lane) to Beauchief (Abbey Lane) – occurred on 28

February 1959. These resulted in the end of trams reversing in Fitzalan Square or Flat Street. The last car from Beauchief to Woodseats was No 199, which was also the last car in service in the old livery and withdrawn following this conversion. The last car from Woodseats to Beauchief was No 274, and the last car from Fitzalan Square to Sheffield Lane Top via Savile Street was No 233. Shoreham Street Depot also closed to trams at this time. Following these conversions, the tram fleet was reduced to 130 by 31 March 1959.

It was announced in late summer 1959 that the next conversions – Wadsley Bridge to Woodseats via either Queen's Road or Shoreham Street – would occur on 3 October 1959. Also affected by the conversion was the workmen's service from Meadowhead to Vulcan Road via Shoreham Street, and the late-night service to and from Meadowhead. The last car to run from Woodseats to Wadsley Bridge

The services from Sheffield Lane Top were converted to bus operation in two stages on 28 February 1959, when those via Savile Street succumbed, and on 2 April 1960, when the services to Woodseats and Meadowhead followed. Here 'Roberts' No 521 makes use of the trolley reverser at the Sheffield Lane Top terminus before heading back south with a service to Meadowhead via Pitsmoor. R. W. A. Jones/Online Transport Archive (SD26)

One of the cars painted in the controversial green livery, No 202, stands at the Woodseats terminus before heading to Wadsley Bridge via Shoreham Street. The last trams operated to Woodseats on this service on 3 October 1959; other routes serving Woodseats were those to Beauchief, converted on 28 February 1959, and to Sheffield Lane Top, converted on 2 April 1960. R. W. A. Jones/Online Transport Archive (SD37)

was No 210, which was becoming a veteran of last duties having done two previously. A further 30 cars were withdrawn following these conversions, reducing the fleet to 100. With the closure of Tinsley Depot, all surviving passenger cars, along with the remaining snow ploughs (destined to be last used on 17 February 1960; when they were advertised for sale in March it was a clear indication that the system was not expected to see a further winter), were allocated to Tenter Street Depot. Thereafter Tinsley Depot was used solely for storing withdrawn cars pending their one-way journey to the Thos W. Ward scrapyard.

The next year, 1960, was the system's last. On 5 March 1960, 40 surplus tramcars were advertised for sale along with six single-deck snow ploughs, 450 tramway poles and 6 miles of overhead. Also in March, the track was singled from Midland Station to Leadmill Street to facilitate the construction of a new traffic island. The penultimate stage occurred on 2 April with the conversion of the Meadowhead to Sheffield Lane Top service. The last car at Meadowhead was No 121 and at Sheffield Lane Top No 100. The 40 cars withdrawn as a consequence of this conversion were Nos 25, 69, 73/75, 83/85/87/89, 98, 121/51/61/70/73/74/

SHEFFIELD
TRANSPORT & JOINT OMNIBUS COMMITTEE

SHEFFIELD CORPORATION
AND
BRITISH RAILWAYS

TRAMWAY & OMNIBUS
TIME TABLE

1st May, 1960 until 30th September, 1960

22

TRAMWAY TIMETABLE

BEAUCHIEF — CITY — VULCAN ROAD
(Beauchief Section)

(…Street)	Cars leave Beauchief for City		
…unday	Mon. to Fri.	Saturday	Sunday
am	am	pm	am	am

(table partly cut off — readable figures include Mon. to Fri. am: 5 1M, 5 12, 5 30M, 5 37, 6 0M, 6 11, 6 22, 6 40, 6 50, 7 3, and at freq. ints. until 8 51, 9 17, and every 30 mins until 3 17; pm: 3 47 and freq. ints. until … Saturday am: 5 1M, 5 12, 5 30M, 5 37, 6 11, 6 27, 6 40, 6 50, 7 3, and at frequent intervals until 9 55, 10 15, 10 25, 10 45, 11 5, 11 17, 11 25, 11 36; Sunday am: 5 5 and every 30 mins until 9 12, and every 15 mins until pm 12 12, and at frequent intervals until 9 55, 10 15, 10 25, 10 47, 11 5, 11 17, 11 25, 11 36)

…ly, additional Cars are operated to … minutes.
…stone Street to Beauchief, 11.45 p.m.
…eauchief to City, 12.10, 12.40, 1.10,
…ulcan Road, Sunday to Friday, 10.47
…eys see Route 61.

23

TRAMWAY TIMETABLE

BEAUCHIEF — CITY — VULCAN ROAD
(Vulcan Road Section)

Cars leave City (High Street) for Vulcan Road				Cars leave Vulcan Road for City		
Mon. to Friday	Saturday	Sunday		Mon. to Friday	Saturday	Sunday
am	am	am	am	am	am	am
3 55	3 55	3 55	10 20	4 29	4 29	4 23
4 30T	4 30T	4 30	and every 15 mins until	4 50T	4 50T	4 57
4 50T	5 5	5 5	12 35	5 10T	5 10T	5 28
5 0	5 7	5 32	and at freq. ints. until	5 23	5 37	5 58
5 14	6 5	6 35	pm	5 44	5 44	6 28
5 22	5 22	6 50		5 56	5 49	6 58
5 28	5 27	7 5		6 6	6 6	7 13
5 35	5 5	7 10		and at frequent intervals until	and at frequent intervals until	7 28
and at frequent intervals until	and at frequent intervals until	7 35		pm	pm	7 33
pm	pm	7 40		11 11	11 18	7 53
10 48	10 48	8 5		11 23	11 23	8 13
11 0	10 58	8 30		11 33	11 31	8 28
11 10	11 8	8 50		11 38	11 38	8 58
11 15	11 15	9 5				9 13
		11 0				9 28
		10 5				9 58
						10 28

am (Sunday, Vulcan Road for City continued): 10 43, 10 58, 11 13, 11 43; pm: 12 3, 12 13, and at freq. ints. until 11 11, 11 33, 11 38

Journey time approximately 22 minutes.
T—*Runs to or from Tinsley (Weedon Street) only.*
Last through car Vulcan Road to Beauchief—10.52 p.m. daily.
For additional late night journeys see Route 69.

The cover of the last Sheffield timetable issued that covered trams for its duration and the relevant pages recording the final services from the city centre to Beauchief and Vulcan Road. Author's Collection

92, 201/06/08/10/19/20/27/30/33/34/ 44/48/51/54/59/65/67/69/70/72/ 79/91/93, 520; No 520 was the first of the Roberts-built cars to succumb. Also withdrawn were works cars Nos 352/57/59/60/64/65; this left only Nos 330/49/50/61 in service. No 354 was purchased by the Tramway Museum Society for restoration as single-deck car No 46. This left sixty trams in service to operate the surviving route Beauchief/

The loop at Millhouses was taken out of service on 29 August 1960. Here No 246 in the new and No 147 in the old liveries make use of the loop while a third car heads south towards Beauchief.
R. W. A. Jones/Online Transport Archive (SD36

Sheffield No 287 pictured at Vulcan Road; although the service to Vulcan Road survived until 8 October 1960 and the final closure, No 287 was withdrawn during the summer of that year. Harry Luff/Online Transport Archive

Millhouses to Vulcan Road/ Weedon Street.

That the system was entering its final months became evident during the summer of 1960 with the frequency of service on the Millhouses-Beauchief section reduced from every 15 minutes to every 30 minutes; the section from Millhouses into the city retained a car every 7$^1/_2$ minutes. On 28 August 1960 the turning loop at Millhouses was closed to permit the construction of a bus turning circle; the replacement trolley reverser caused initial teething problems when first used. Between 1 June and 30 September a further 19 cars were withdrawn from service – Nos 68, 72, 100/50, 221/52/56/80/87/98, 430/83 and 505/11/21/25/31-33 – leaving 41 in stock. No 349 was also withdrawn and sent to Queen's Road for conversion into an illuminated car for the closing ceremony. The majority of these cars

made their way to the scrapyard on either 12 or 13 August; four of the Roberts-built cars – Nos 511/12/25/33 – succumbed as a result of requiring new tyres. During August two other Roberts cars, Nos 510/13, had been transferred to Queen's Road Works for repainting in the special commemorative liveries to mark the closure. The number in service was further reduced on 7 October with the withdrawal of Nos 508 and 524, both of which developed faults and which were despatched to Tinsley Depot in the company of Nos 330 and 350.

The final day of service for Sheffield's trams was 8 October 1960 when thirty-nine cars were in theory available for service, although only twenty-seven – Nos 97, 102/12/15/22/67/83, 222/23/58/64/81/96, 501/02/06/09/14-17/19/22/26/28/35/36 – were used. With the exception of No 264 (which was scheduled for preservation), all cars terminated their final duties at Tinsley where they were taken into the depot to facilitate their later transfer to Ward's scrapyard. No 502 was the last service car to Beauchief in theory, although No 222, which was the last service car to depart from Vulcan Road, ran unscheduled to Beauchief where it arrived fully loaded and with no space for any passengers wishing to board at Beauchief for the centre. No 517 was the last service car at Vulcan Road, and, appropriately, No 536 was the last car to enter service from Tenter Street Depot. The last car to arrive at Tinsley was No 504 at 6.19 pm. The final procession departed from Tenter Street at 6.3 pm and was formed, in sequence, by Nos 349 (the illuminated car), 46 (now restored), 189, 503/04/07/18/21/23/27/29/30/34/13/10. This was, however, not quite the final movement for Sheffield's trams as, between then and 21 December 1960, cars made their final journey from Tinsley Depot to the scrapyard. The last to make the trip was, again appropriately, No 536, which was accompanied by the general manager, chairman of the transport committee and 95-year-old Frank Simpkin, who had helped to push out the first horse tram from Tinsley Depot in the nineteenth century.

Even this was not the end of the Sheffield tram story for, on 3 December 1961, restored horse car No 15 was used along a short stretch of surviving track at the Moor to celebrate the switching on of the city's Christmas lights.

Sheffield Depots

As with Leeds, the size of the Sheffield system dictated that it had a number of tramway depots. The main works, which had also served as a running shed until 1929, was at Queen's Road south of the city centre; this retained tramway maintenance work until the system's closure on 8 October 1960. Other tramway depots were: Holme Lane, situated on the branch to Malin Bridge and close to Hillsborough football ground, which ceased to be a tram depot on 23 April 1954; Crookes, on Crookes Road, which lost its allocation on 5 May 1957 with the closure of the route to Crookes; Shoreham Street, sited to the south of the city centre at the junction of the lines running along Shoreham Street and Suffolk Road, which ceased to accommodate trams on 28 February 1959; Tinsley, located towards the terminus of the route towards Tinsley, which ceased to be a running shed on 3 October 1959, but was used for storing trams before scrapping through to the system's closure; and, in the city centre, Tenter Street, served by track off the route to Middlewood, which survived as a tram depot until the system's closure on 8 October 1960. There had also been a depot at the terminus of the Nether Edge route, but this had closed with the route in 1934.

Sheffield Closures

12 December 1948
Vulcan Road-Templeborough

5 January 1952
Fulwood-Malin Bridge (via Hunters Bar)

27 March 1954
Ecclesall-Middlewood

7 April 1956
Walkley-Intake

4 May 1957
Crookes-Handsworth

26 October 1957
Exchange Street-Sheffield Lane Top (via Newhall Street)

4 January 1958
Furnival Street and Paternoster Row

12 April 1958
Intake (Elm Tree)-Fitzalan Square via Prince of Wales Road

6 December 1958
Brightside-Savile Street and Fitzalan Square; factory-hours service Brightside-Sheffield Lane Top (via Upwell Street and Firth Park)

28 February 1959
Fitzalan Square-Sheffield Lane Top (via Savile Street); Beauchief-Woodseats (via Abbey Lane)

3 October 1959
Wadsley Bridge-Woodseats; peak-hours workmen's service Vulcan Road-Meadowhead (via Shoreham Street)

2 April 1960
Sheffield Lane Top-Woodseats/Meadowhead

8 October 1960
Beauchief/Millhouses-Weedon Street/Vulcan Road

Sheffield Fleet

1-35

No 1 was the last tram delivered to Sheffield by local manufacturer Cravens Railway Carriage & Wagon; new in 1927,

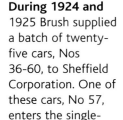

No 3, one of the thirty-four cars built at Queen's Road between 1928 and 1930, recorded in the original dark blue livery at Meadowhead on 22 May 1949.
Michael H. Waller

During 1924 and 1925 Brush supplied a batch of twenty-five cars, Nos 36-60, to Sheffield Corporation. One of these cars, No 57, enters the single-track section along Nursery Street on the Wadsley Bridge to Woodseats route.
R. W. A Jones/Online Transport Archive (SD23)

it was followed between 1928 and 1930 with thirty cars of a similar design built in the corporation's own workshops. All had fully enclosed bodies and were fitted with Peckham P22 trucks. Nos 25 and 27

received modified lower saloons as part of work undertaken on the 'Standard' cars in the early 1950s and these two survived in service until 1960; the remaining cars of this series were withdrawn between 1951 and 1957.

36-60

These twenty-five cars were supplied during 1924, and 1925 and were fitted with Brush fully enclosed bodies on Peckham P22 trucks. All were withdrawn between 1950 and 1957.

61-130 (except Nos 83/85, 100/12/19/29)

Built in the corporation's workshops between 1930 and 1933, these seventy fully enclosed trams were fitted with Peckham P22 trucks. Six of the type, Nos 83/85, 100/12/19/29, were destroyed by enemy action during the Second World War and were replaced by the cars built between 1941 and 1944. A number of the type – Nos 68/69, 72/73/75, 87/89, 97/98, 102/15/22/28 – had their lower saloons

One of the seventy fully enclosed cars built between 1930 and 1933, No 110 is seen heading towards Darnall. The service from Fitzalan Square to Darnall was converted to bus operation on 12 April 1958.
Harry Luff/Online Transport Archive (T512)

rebuilt between 1952 and 1956. The cars were withdrawn between 1951 and 1960.

131-155 (except No 133)

Although the majority of the 210 fully enclosed 'Standard' trams delivered between 1928 and 1936 were built in Queen's Road, a single batch of twenty-five was built with bodies supplied by

Sheffield 'Standard' No 132 is pictured at Millhouses. This was one of the batch of twenty-five supplied to the corporation by W. & E. Hill Ltd during 1929 and 1930. All were withdrawn for scrap between 1956 and 1960.
R. W. A Jones/Online Transport Archive (SD35)

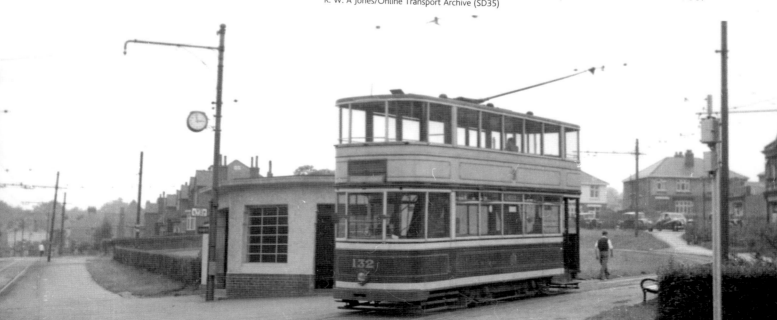

One of the 'Standard' cars built at Queen's Road between 1933 and 1936, No 167 was one of seven that received rebuilt lower decks during the early 1950s.
A. C. Crichton/Hamish Stevenson Collection/Online Transport Archive

and were delivered between 1933 and 1936. Three cars – Nos 192, 201/27 – were casualties of enemy action during the Second World War, and seven – Nos 161/67/70/73/74/83/91 – had their lower decks rebuilt as part of the programme undertaken in the early 1950s. All were withdrawn between 1958 and 1960; No 189 was preserved on withdrawal and is now part of the collection at the National Tramway Museum.

231-42/49-303 (except Nos 261/74)

Between 1936 and 1939, 67 'Improved Standard' cars were built at Queen's Road on Peckham P22 trucks. Two of the type – Nos 261 and 274 – were destroyed as a result of enemy action during the Second World War. The remaining sixty-five cars survived until they were withdrawn between 1957 and 1960. Following withdrawal, No 264 was preserved and is now part of the National Tramway Museum collection.

W. &. E. Hill Ltd on Peckham P22 trucks. No 133 was destroyed as a result of enemy action during the Second World War, and No 151 was one of the cars to see its lower saloon rebuilt during the early 1950s. Delivered originally during 1929 and 1930, the twenty-four surviving cars were taken out of service between 1956 and 1960.

156-230/43-48 (except Nos 192, 201/27)

These 'Standard' cars were built at Queen's Road on Peckham P22 trucks

311-24

In 1941 Sheffield acquired a batch of fourteen cars second-hand from Newcastle. The cars had been Newcastle Nos 122/24/13/29/18/17/14/16/12/

One of the sixty-five 'Improved Standard', also known as 'Domed Roof' Standards, cars to survive the war, No 288 is seen in the company of 'Roberts' car No 503 at Intake on 13 August 1950. The Intake route was converted to bus operation on 8 April 1956.
R. W. A. Jones/Online Transport Archive (SD6)

During the war Sheffield Corporation acquired two batches of second-hand trams to supplement the fleet at a time when it had suffered severe damage from the Luftwaffe. The first to arrive were fourteen cars, Nos 311-24, that had been bought from Newcastle upon Tyne Corporation in 1941. Fully enclosed before entering service in Sheffield, the cars survived until withdrawal by 1952. No 323 was originally Newcastle No 123.
F. E. J. Ward/Online Transport Archive (20)

19/25/26/23/24 respectively and were originally delivered as open-top four-wheel cars in 1901. The original bodies were supplied by Hurst Nelson and fitted on Brill 21E trucks. All were rebuilt as fully enclosed in Sheffield during 1941 and 1942 before entering service, and Nos 311 and 313 also received slightly longer replacement trucks. The ex-Newcastle cars were withdrawn between 1948 and 1952. The body of No 317 (ex-Newcastle 114) was subsequently rescued and, following restoration, now forms part of the fleet at Beamish.

325-334

In 1942 a further batch of second-hand trams was acquired, this time from Bradford. Originally delivered to Bradford during 1920 and 1921, and fitted with open-balcony English Electric bodies on Brill 21E trucks, the ten cars were originally Bradford Nos 214/43/42/16/ 37/51/57/15/19/17. Before entering service in Sheffield, the cars were regauged from Bradford's 4ft 0in to standard gauge and rebuilt as fully enclosed. The ten cars were taken

out of service during 1950 and 1951, at which time No 330 was converted into a single-deck works car. As such, No 330 survived until 1960 and was preserved

In 1942 Sheffield acquired ten trams second-hand from Bradford Corporation. Nos 325-34 were regauged from Bradford's 4ft 0in gauge to standard gauge before entering service and were also provided with enclosed balconies in place of the open balconies used in Bradford. No 331 had originally been Bradford No 257. All withdrawn by 1951, one of the batch – No 330 – was cut down to single deck for works duties and was ultimately preserved. F. N. T. Lloyd-Jones/Online Transport Archive

During the
Second World
War, fourteen
Sheffield trams
were destroyed by
enemy action. They
were all replaced
between 1941
and 1944. One of
the fourteen cars
built as a wartime
replacement was
No 201.
A. C. Crichton/Hamish
Stevenson Collection/Online

83/85, 100/12/19/29/33/92, 201/27/61/74, 430/83

During the Second World War,
Sheffield, as a major centre of the steel
industry, was an inevitable target for the
Luftwaffe and the city suffered severe
raids. The city's transport network
was not immune to the damage and,
during the war, a number of trams were
destroyed. The most devastating losses
occurred during the massive raid of 12
December when fourteen cars (as listed
above) were destroyed. Between 1941
and 1944 all fourteen were replaced by
'Improved Standards' with bodies built
at Queen's Road on Peckham P22 trucks.
The wartime replacement cars remained
in service until withdrawal between
1957 and 1960.

on withdrawal; it now forms part of the
National Tramway Museum collection.

336/39/42-50

In 1907 a batch of open-balcony cars, Nos
258-272, was delivered. The bodies were
supplied by UEC on M&G radial trucks,
but the latter were replaced by Peckham
P22s between 1918 and 1920. No 259 was
rebuilt as fully enclosed in 1911, with the
remainder following between 1924 and
1927. In 1937 the batch was renumbered
336-50, but Nos 337/38/40/41 were
withdrawn from service by the end of
1939. The remaining eleven cars survived
in passenger service until withdrawal
between 1947 and 1954; on withdrawal
No 346 operated as a driver training car
until 1957, No 349 as a stores car until
1960 and No 350 as a snowplough, also
until 1960. No 350 had been withdrawn
on 19 March 1953. Its conversion to
snowplough use was the last conversion
of a passenger car to works use
undertaken in Sheffield. No 342 was
secured for preservation. After spending
some time in the museum at Clapham,
it passed eventually to Beamish and,
after some years, was fully restored as
Sheffield No 264.

352-365

Between 1920 and 1933 Sheffield
converted fourteen old passenger cars
into snowploughs. Nos 353/55 were
converted from horse snowploughs
Nos 274/76 and were withdrawn in
March 1952, and Nos 352/54/56-65
were converted from electric cars Nos
172, 46, 185, 225/26, 111/13, 99, 39, 42,
73/77. All were withdrawn between
1952 and 1960; No 354 – originally No
46 (a single-deck car with G. F. Milnes
& Co body on a Peckham Cantilever
truck dating to 1899) – was preserved.
Fully restored to its original condition
for the closure in 1960, No 46 is now
part of the National Tramway Museum
collection.

CROOKES SCHOOL RD

343

One of the eleven surviving cars supplied in 1907 by UEC, No 343 is seen outside Crookes Depot. Originally delivered with M&G radial trucks, the trams received replacement Peckham P22s between 1918 and 1920. All were withdrawn from passenger service by 1954, and Crookes Depot closed its doors to trams three years later. R. W. A Jones/Online Transport Archive (SD4)

Three of the fleet's works cars – Nos 354, 330 and 349 – await their next duties. Of the three, two – Nos 354 (now restored as No 46) and 330 – survive in preservation; No 349, which was used as a stores car until 1960, was scrapped, but sister car No 342 was preserved.
A. C. Crichton/Hamish Stevenson Collection/Online Transport Archive

366-69

Four experimental fully enclosed trams were constructed in Queen's Road on Peckham P22 trucks between 1918 and 1921. This quartet formed the basis of the 150 cars – Nos 36-60, 376-500 – that were delivered between 1919 and 1927. The four experimental cars survived until withdrawal in the 1950s.

370

A further experimental car, No 370, was constructed in Queen's Road on a Peckham P22 truck in 1931. It was similar to the Standard class of Nos 2-35, 61-230/42-48, but was of aluminium rather than steel construction and so was much lighter. As a result it was fitted with forty rather than the more usual 50hp motors. No 370 was withdrawn from service in 1957.

371-75

Between 1933 and 1937 five older trams

Sheffield No 366 was one of four experimental fully enclosed trams delivered between 1918 and 1921. It is seen here entering the loop at Millhouses with 'Standard' No 24 behind on Abbeydale Road South. The loop at Millhouses was removed at the end of August 1960. R. W. A. Jones/Online Transport Archive (SD34)

A final experimental tram, No 370, was constructed in Queen's Road in 1931. Constructed with an aluminium, rather than steel, body, it was considerably lighter than the 'Standard' cars. Marcus Eavis/Online Transport Archive

Between 1919 and 1927, 125 fully enclosed cars on Peckham P22 trucks were supplied to Sheffield by Brush and Cravens. One of the Cravens-built examples, No 489, is pictured on Abbeydale Road.
R. W. A. Jones/Online Transport Archive (SD18)

were renumbered for works duties. These were two old electric cars – Nos 371 and 372 that were ex-211/12 in 1933 and acted as water cars – and three ex-horse cars that had been converted to electric operation between 1901 and 1907. No 371 was withdrawn in 1951 when its equipment was transferred to ex-Bradford No 330 (withdrawn on 11 April 1951 from passenger service), which was cut down to single-deck for its new role. No 372 had been withdrawn during the war when its truck had been transferred to

one of the ex-Newcastle cars, but its body was not scrapped until December 1950. No 373 had been horse car No 8 of 1897 and had been converted to a salt car in 1906; it became a stores car, No 279, in 1919 and was renumbered 373 in 1937. It was withdrawn in 1951. No 374 dated originally to 1877 and had been converted to a salt car in 1904. Converted to a stores car as No 280 in 1918, it became No 374 in 1937 and was withdrawn in December 1951 when it was replaced by No 349, which had been withdrawn from passenger service on 22 January 1951 and re-entered service as a works car on 28 March 1951. No 374 survived, however, until being sent to Wards for scrap on 14 June 1956. No 375 was originally horse car No 15 of 1874; it became breakdown car No 166 in 1902 and was renumbered 375 in 1937. Withdrawn in 1946, it was restored as a horse car for the fiftieth anniversary of municipal operation and survived until final closure. As No 15 the car now forms part of the National Tramway Museum collection.

376-500 (except Nos 430 and 483)

These were fully enclosed cars delivered between 1919 and 1927. All were fitted with Peckham P22 trucks with bodies supplied by Brush (Nos 376-450) or Cravens (Nos 451-500). Two of the cars, Nos 430 and 483, were destroyed by enemy action during the Second World War and No 493 was withdrawn in 1946 – the first of the post-First World War-built trams to be withdrawn other than as a result of wartime damage. The remaining cars were withdrawn between 1950 and 1957. In November 1951, as a result of an administrative error, No 465 was sent for scrap in place of No 413. The body of No 413 was transferred to the truck of No 465 and operated as No 465 thereafter. Although none were preserved when withdrawn, the lower deck of Cravens-built No 460 has been subsequently rescued and is now based at the Sheffield Transport Museum.

501

In 1946 Sheffield introduced its first post-war car, No 501, following its construction in Queen's Road – the last new tram to be constructed in the works. Fitted with an M&T Hornless Type 588 four-wheel truck, No 501 was the only Sheffield tram to be fitted with fluorescent lighting. As 1946 marked the fiftieth anniversary of the corporation's

In 1946 Sheffield Corporation built a new four-wheel car in its works at Queen's Road; numbered 501, the car was the prototype for the later Roberts-built cars, although there were minor detail differences between the prototype and the production cars. No 501 is seen here on Parkside Road during a Southern Counties Touring Society tour on 21 August 1949.
John Meredith/Online Transport Archive (82/11)

takeover of the city's tramway network, it was inevitable that No 501 would become known as the 'Jubilee' car. No 501 survived until 1960 but was scrapped after withdrawal.

A. C. Crichton/Hamish
Stevenson Collection/Online
Transport Archive

By the time that the last of the thirty-five Roberts-built cars were delivered, the fate of the Sheffield system was already decided with the result that the trams, such as No 532, had an operational life of less than a decade.

502-36

The thirty-five 'Roberts' cars were delivered between 1950 and 1952, and were built by Charles H. Roberts & Co Ltd of Horbury. They were constructed on M&T Hornless type 588 trucks and represented the only double-deck trams built by Roberts. They were also the last traditional four-wheel trams constructed for any first-generation tramway in Britain. Based around the design of No 501, but with differences – such as the use of a steel frame rather than one of composite construction – the whole class survived until withdrawal in 1960. Two, Nos 510/13, received special commemorative liveries to mark the system's closure in October 1960 and were subsequently preserved. No 510, which retains its special livery, is part of the National Tramway Museum collection, and No 513, now in standard livery, is on loan at the East Anglian Transport Museum from Beamish.

SOUTH SHIELDS

Although the standard-gauge system at South Shields had acquired a modern streamlined car, No 52, in 1936, powers to operate trolleybuses had been obtained in August 1935. Initially it was intended that trolleybuses would supplement, rather than replace, the trams, but the policy soon changed to one of tramcar replacement. One route – the long service from Moon Street to The Ridgeway, Cleadon, with its extensive stretch of reserved track along the **King George Road** (the Cleadon Light Railway) – was, however, **to** be retained. The fleet, reduced from its peak number of forty-nine in 1931 to thirteen at the start of 1945, was housed at Dean Road depot. One of the closed routes, that to Ocean Road, was restored for a period between 25 January 1943 and 18 December 1943, when it was replaced by a new trolleybus service. South Shields suffered wartime damage, with the loss of three trolleybuses and one motorbus. After the war, the surviving trams operated until 31 March 1946; the official closing ceremony took place on the following day **when No 39, t**he surviving car of a batch of five delivered in 1914, carried the official party. With the exception of No

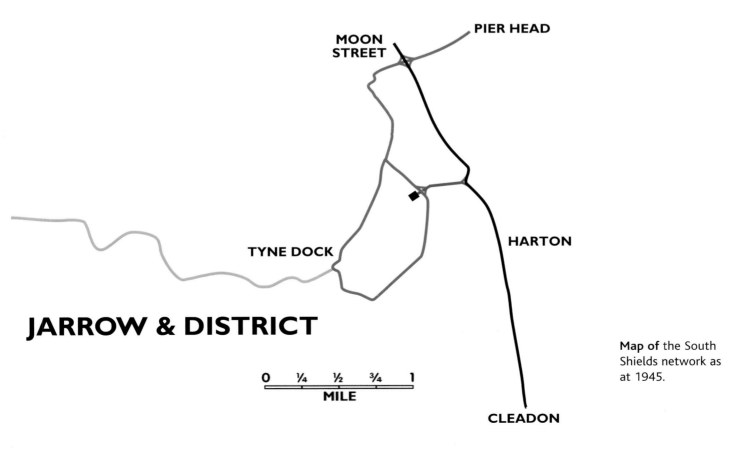

SOUTH SHIELDS

PIER HEAD

MOON STREET

HARTON

TYNE DOCK

JARROW & DISTRICT

0   ¼   ½   ¾   1
MILE

CLEADON

Map of the South Shields network as at 1945.

52, sold to Sunderland, all the surviving cars were scrapped after closure.

South Shields Depot

Following the pre-war closures, South Shields tram depot, Dean Road, was located away from the sole surviving route – Moon Street to The Ridgeway – and so was accessed via track no longer used by passenger services from Westoe along Dean Road. By 1945 the system's needs had meant that only part of the site accommodated tramcars and this

requirement ceased on 31 March 1946 with the closure of the system.

South Shields Closure

31 March 1946
Moon Street-The Ridgeway

South Shields Fleet

16

No 16 was one of two cars acquired from Ayr Corporation in 1932. Originally supplied as open-balcony cars built with English Electric bodies on Preston P22 four-wheel trucks to Dumbarton in 1921 as Nos 31 and 32, the pair were sold to Ayr in 1929 as Nos 29 and 30. The two were numbered 54 and 57 when first operated in South Shields, but were

No 16 was the one surviving car of a duo acquired from Ayr Corporation in 1932; with the Wouldhave Memorial as a backdrop, this pre-war view sees No 16 rebuilt as fully enclosed in 1934 awaiting departure with a service to Stanhope Road. The Stanhope Road route was converted to trolleybus operation in March 1937. Barry Cross Collection/Online Transport Archive

South Shields No 51 was one of four ex-Wigan Corporation trams acquired in 1932 that survived into the war. It is pictured here heading south over the route towards the Ridgeway.
F. K. Farrell Collection/Online Transport Archive

renumbered 16 and 34 in 1934 when they were fitted with Hurst Nelson 21E trucks; No 16 was also rebuilt as fully enclosed in 1934. The surviving car was withdrawn in 1946 for scrap.

23, 33, 50/51

In 1932 South Shields acquired six trams second-hand from Wigan. Four of the trams were rebuilt as fully enclosed by South Shields between 1932 and 1935; the remaining two, Wigan Nos 3 and 5, did not enter service. Nos 23, 33, 50/51 were originally Wigan Nos 4, 2, 6 and 1 respectively; No 33 was renumbered from 52 in 1935. The quartet had English Electric-built bodies on Brill 43E bogies and survived until withdrawal in 1945 (Nos 33 and 50) or 1946 (Nos 23 and 51).

39

No 39 was one of a batch of five cars, Nos 36-40, that was supplied originally in 1914 with open-balcony Brush bodies on Peckham P22 four-wheel trucks. In 1931 No 39 was rebuilt as fully enclosed, the only one of the batch to be so treated, and survived until 1946.

41-45

This batch of fully enclosed cars was supplied in 1921. The five cars were fitted with English Electric bodies and Brill 76E bogies. Originally the five were fitted with front exits, but these were removed

from all except No 43. The quintet survived until withdrawal in 1946.

52

In 1936 South Shields acquired a single modern tram – the streamlined No 52. This was supplied with a streamlined centre-entrance body by Brush on M&T swing-link bogies. On withdrawal in 1946, it was sold for further service with Sunderland.

SOUTH YORKSHIRE SUPERTRAM

Parliamentary approval for the construction of the Supertram network was obtained in 1985 and the 18-mile system was opened in stages during 1994 and 1995. The first section to open was Fitzalan Square to Meadowhall on 21 March 1994; this was followed by Fitzalan Square to Spring Lane (22 August 1994), Spring Lane to Gleadless Townend (5 December 1994), Fitzalan Square to Cathedral (18 February 1995), Cathedral to Shalesmoor (17 February 1995), Gleadless Townend

to Halfway (27 March 1995), Gleadless Townend to Herdings Park (3 April 1995) and Shalesmoor to Middlewood and Malin Bridge (23 October 1995).

Originally the system was operated by a subsidiary of South Yorkshire PTE, but this was sold to Stagecoach in 1997 and, since then, Stagecoach has operated and maintained the system on a concession.

South Yorkshire Supertram Depot

The Sheffield Supertram network currently possesses a single running

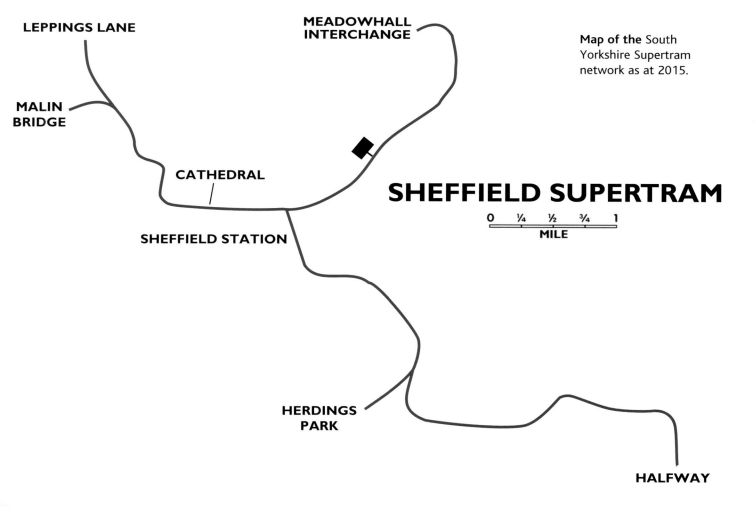

Map of the South Yorkshire Supertram network as at 2015.

SHEFFIELD SUPERTRAM

0   ¼   ½   ¾   1
MILE

LEPPINGS LANE

MALIN BRIDGE

MEADOWHALL INTERCHANGE

CATHEDRAL

SHEFFIELD STATION

HERDINGS PARK

HALFWAY

shed, Nunnery, which opened on 21
March 1994 and is located on the site of
the erstwhile Nunnery engine shed in
Sheffield.

South Yorkshire Supertram Fleet
01-25 (later 101-25)
To operate the new system, twenty-
five articulated single-deck trams were
acquired from Siemens-Duewag of
Düsseldorf in Germany. Delivered in
1992, the new trams initially operated in
a light grey with dark blue livery with
Supertram fleetnames. In 1997, following
Stagecoach's acquisition of the franchise
to operate the system, the trams appeared
in standard Stagecoach livery. Following
refurbishment of the fleet between 2006
and 2009, a new predominantly blue
livery was adopted. A further upgrading
programme began in 2009 and all twenty-
five cars remain in service at the time of
writing.

SUNDERLAND

n Charles Anthony Hopkins, appointed general manager in May 1929, Sunderland possessed one of the most pro-tram managers of the interwar years. Under his control, the operator saw considerable investment in its fleet through the rebuilding of existing cars, along with the acquisition of both new and second-hand trams. At the end of the war, the fleet numbered more than eighty

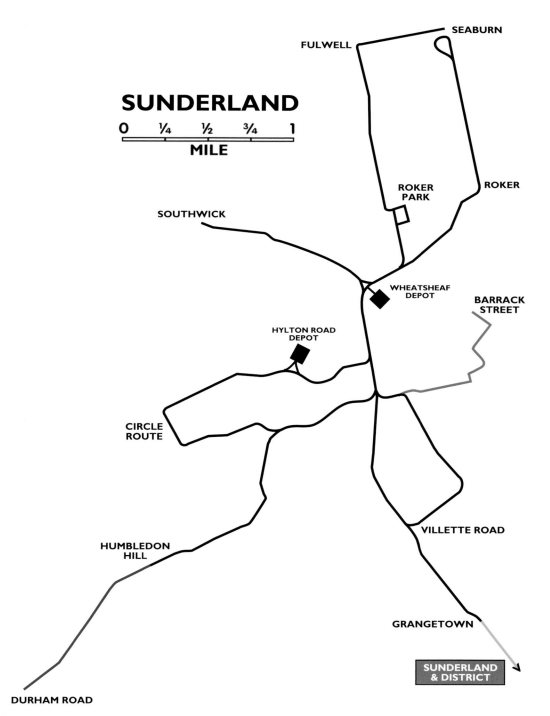

SUNDERLAND

0	¼	½	¾	1

MILE

SEABURN

FULWELL

ROKER PARK

ROKER

SOUTHWICK

WHEATSHEAF DEPOT

BARRACK STREET

HYLTON ROAD DEPOT

CIRCLE ROUTE

VILLETTE ROAD

HUMBLEDON HILL

GRANGETOWN

SUNDERLAND & DISTRICT

DURHAM ROAD

Map of the Sunderland network as at 1945.

trams, including four new streamlined cars delivered between 1938 and 1940.

Apart from the Barrack Street route, converted to bus operation in 1924, the entire corporation network was intact at the start of 1945, although the coastal section from Roker to Seaburn was suspended from 15 December 1939 and replaced by a bus service. The suspended service was reinstated on 4 June 1945. At about the same time, No 61, which had been stored for some years in a semi-derelict condition in the works at Hylton Road, re-entered service.

That the tram was perceived as having a future in Sunderland was also evinced by the decision in early 1945 to double a stretch of 443yd of the Durham Road route at a cost of £7,000, along with repair work to track on Ryhope Road. Later the same year the Transport Committee accepted a quotation of £1,030 from Titan Trackwork Co Ltd for the rebuilding of the junction between Villette Road and Ryhope Road. This reinstated a junction that had been abandoned originally in 1929 and subsequently removed. Its reinstatement permitted the introduction of a peak-hour circular service in April 1946. This service was, however, not successful and ceased in July 1946, when the junction again effectively became moribund. Further trackwork saw the relaying of the loop that served Roker Park and the removal of a crossover in Gladstone Street. Other work saw the continued conversion of the fleet from bow collector to pantograph operation, with a number of cars – including Nos 13 and 63 – so treated. (Sunderland had begun the process of converting its tramcar fleet to bow collector operation in 1931 before switching to pantographs three years later. The process of conversion to pantograph operation was completed in 1948.) The first proposals for the extension of the Hambledon Hill route surfaced towards the end of 1945, and at the end of the year a tender from

Hadfields for the relaying of the track between Hylton Road and Trimdon Street, and at the Southwick terminus, was accepted.

If the preceding suggested that everything was rosy, this was not the case. In February 1946 Hopkins was requested to prepare a report on the future of the tramways. Although conversion was an option, so too was retention and development. Despite this straw in the wind, authorisation was given in early 1946 for the purchase of eighteen new traction columns, and doubling of the route from Ettrick Grove to the Hambledon Hill terminus was in hand. The fleet was further strengthened by the restoration of Nos 99 and 100 to regular service; these were added to later the same year with the purchase of South Shields' sole streamlined car, No 52, that became No 48 on Wearside. Following the closure of the South Shields system, Sunderland also acquired track salvaged from the Cleadon route and other material.

For 1946, the Transport Department was authorised to spend £9,000 on the doubling of the Hambledon Hill route, £1,539 to the extension of Fulwell Depot and £2,118 on other track repairs. At the same time a new ticketing system, the Ultimate, was under test; this method of ticketing, however, was not introduced to Sunderland until 1966, long after the trams had ceased operation. That trams still had a future was confirmed in mid-1945 when the new council voted 58 to 1 (the one opponent being Councillor Cairns) to authorise the extension of the Hambledon Hill route along the Durham Road. An application for a Light Railway Order for the extension was lodged in early 1947. At about the same time, Hopkins reported on the future of the system. He concluded: 'I fail to see any reason for the scrapping of a system giving such excellent service.' He did, however, provide costs for possible conversion, including the purchase of

184 new buses for £714,000.

Taking advantage of tramway abandonment elsewhere, Sunderland acquired six second-hand trams from Manchester and one from Bury during 1947; these were the last trams that Sunderland acquired. During 1947 work progressed on the first 630yd section of the Durham Road extension; constructed on sleeper track located in the central reservation of the road, this extension opened on 21 February 1948, and work was in progress for a further 673yd extension. This final extension opened on 7 February 1949. By this date, however, Hopkins, who had overseen the development of the Sunderland system for two decades, was dead. He had died on 16 October 1948, to be succeeded by W. H. Snowball, who was another tramway proponent.

By now even Sunderland was feeling the pressure for conversion; in early 1950

During reconstruction work on the railway bridge on Southwick Road, a shuttle service was operated from the railway bridge to Southwick terminus. Here ex-Accrington No 19 is pictured at the temporary terminus with the crossover amended and the outward track severed. The route was converted to bus operation on 2 September 1951 when the decision not to reinstate the full tram service was implemented.
R. W. A. Jones/Online Transport Archive (SN35)

the decision was made to convert the tramway system to bus operation. At an event held in August 1950 to mark the fiftieth anniversary of electric tramcar operation, the chairman of the Transport Committee, Councillor George Lumsden, explained succinctly the rationale: 'Sheer economics has driven the council to agree to their [the trams] substitution.' The first route to succumb, after several delays, was the Villette Road route, which was converted to bus operation on 5 November 1950. The last car to operate over the route was No 81. The cost of conversion was an estimated £12,000 for new buses and £10,000 to reinstate the road. A terminal stub was retained outside the Gas Office. Following the closure, the Grangetown trams were linked to Southwick and a new Fawcett Street-Fulwell service was introduced.

Although the future of the system was now in considerable doubt, there was still evidence that the trams might have a short-term future. In March 1951 the railway bridge on the Southwick route required replacement; although there were rumours this might result in the route's conversion, trams maintained a shuttle service. Ex-Bury No 85 was repainted, and No 35, damaged in an accident on the Durham Road route in October 1950, was repaired and restored to service, as was No 100 that had recently suffered fire damage. Moreover Hadfields had received an order for a replacement set of points.

During the course of 1951, as work

progressed on the new railway bridge on the Southwick route, the cost of reinstating the full tram service was deemed prohibitive with the result that the route was converted to bus operation, suddenly, on 2 September 1951. Following this closure, the Grangetown trams terminated at the Wheat Sheaf.

Snowball did not survive long as general manager. He died on 1 January 1952 and was succeeded by Norman Morton on 1 July 1952. During this six-month gap, Stanley Finkle took over as acting general manager. By the date of Snowball's death tramway abandonment was Council policy, although it was not certain how long the process would take. Borough Engineer J. E. Lewis stated that conversion would be completed by 1971 at the earliest; the reality, however, was a much shorter time frame as the pages of *The Modern Tramway* for the period

One of the ex-Huddersfield cars, No 32, stands at the terminus at Grangetown. The terminus here was modified in 1926 when the roadside reserved track was installed.
R. W. A. Jones/Online Transport Archive (SN16)

reflected. Approval for the Southwick conversion was given at a cost of £16,500 for road reinstatement (less the value of any scrap recovered) plus £12,000 for new buses. The action was approved by the chairman of the Northern Area Licensing Authority, S. W. Nelson, on 29 January 1952. He commented: 'We particularly hope that your Corporation will soon replace trams with buses in Fawcett Street.' Given that Fawcett Street was the main thoroughfare south of the Wear through which trams operated, there was no better indication of official attitudes to the future of the tram in Sunderland. Another indication was that trams Nos 99 and 100 were put up for sale.

In September 1952 it was agreed that conversion would be accelerated with final abandonment coming over a two-year period. A number of factors were behind this, most notably that track required significant investment on the Circle and Grangetown routes, along with the cost of maintaining a mixed fleet. The first indication of the new policy came on 20 September 1952 when buses replaced trams on the football specials to Roker Park. The loop serving the ground survived, however, until final closure as a means of turning trams. The next route to succumb was that to Grangetown, which was last operated by trams on 30 November 1952, with No 74 being the last car to operate over it.

The early part of 1953 saw greater evidence that the system was living on borrowed time. Vehicle and track maintenance was reduced and, in January, No 87 became the last car to undergo a full repaint. Mass withdrawals also started, and by summer the fleet had been reduced to forty-nine with one works car. The majority of withdrawn cars were sold for scrap to a Benton-based merchant. The withdrawn cars were initially taken to Hylton Road where they were dismantled and any usable spares retained for future use; the remains then transferred to

The Circle route via Hylton Road was converted to bus operation on 3 January 1954. Here 1935-built streamlined car No 54 is pictured on Hylton Road This tram was withdrawn shortly after this route was abandoned.
R. W. A. Jones/Online Transport Archive (SN62)

Benton. Among the casualties were the more modern cars as it was decided that the trams that would survive to the end were the ex-Ilford, the ex-Huddersfield and Nos 87-99. The retained cars were all air-braked for operation of the steeply-graded Durham Road route. The fleet in August 1953 totalled 46: Nos 3-9, 13, 22-25, 30-38, 41/42/48/49, 52/53, 63, 71/72/78, 80/83/85/87-98 plus Nos 2, 43 (breakdown car), 55, 86 and 100 that were not in service A further thirty awaited scrapping (including Nos 14-21/26-29, 39, 40/45/46, 50/51/54, 84 and 99). The last car to receive attention to its paintwork in the paint shops was No 42; after work finished on this car the paint shop was demolished.

The next routes converted to bus operation, following the delivery of thirty-seven new buses in late 1953, were the Circle and Seaburn via Roker, both of which succumbed on 3 January 1954,

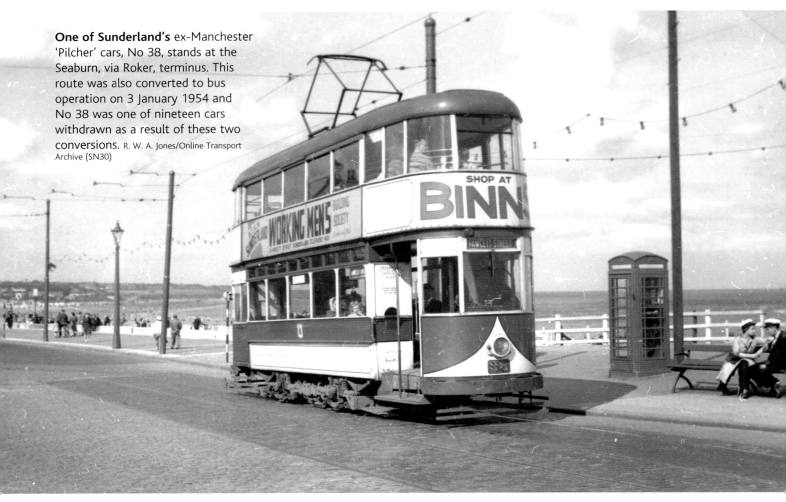

One of Sunderland's ex-Manchester 'Pilcher' cars, No 38, stands at the Seaburn, via Roker, terminus. This route was also converted to bus operation on 3 January 1954 and No 38 was one of nineteen cars withdrawn as a result of these two conversions. R. W. A. Jones/Online Transport Archive (SN30)

The last extension opened in Sunderland was that along the Durham Road; here the ex-MET prototype 'Feltham' car, No 100, leads a line-up of trams on the route. The Durham Road line was the penultimate conversion in Sunderland, succumbing on 28 March 1954. No 100 did not survive until the system's closure, being withdrawn – for preservation – in 1951. R. W. A. Jones/Online Transport Archive (SN21)

having been delayed from 2 November 1953 as a result of the late delivery of the replacement buses. The last car to Seaburn was No 85. As a result of this conversion a further nineteen cars –

Nos 13, 22/23/25, 37/38, 41/42/48/49, 53/55, 63, 71/72/78, 83/88 and 92 – were withdrawn with twenty cars sold to a Stratford-upon-Avon scrap merchant and scrapped at Roker. The fleet now comprised twenty-nine cars – Nos 2-9, seven of the ex-Huddersfield cars and Nos 86/87/89-91/93-8 plus Nos 24, 80/85 – as the department sought permission to convert the last route – Durham Road-Seaburn. The penultimate closure was the route to Durham Road, part of which was only five or six years old, which saw its last trams on 28 March 1954. The last car over the route was ex-Ilford No 8. Withdrawn following this conversion were Nos 3, 4, 6-9, 85 and 94. The chairman of the Transport Committee, Councillor T. W. Atkinson, announced that the estimated cost of the complete abandonment, when finished, would be £500,000; this, no doubt, included the £13,352 to remove

the track from Durham Road and the £37,798 to convert Wheatsheaf Depot to bus operation.

Following the withdrawal of the Durham Road route, the surviving service to Seaburn terminated outside the museum on the short remaining stub of the Villette Road route. Final closure came on 1 October 1954. At 11.20 pm the final procession left for Seaburn; six cars – Nos 24, 31/32/34/35 and 93 – carried the general public, and No 91 conveyed the band, No 96 invited guests and No 86 – suitably bedecked – carried the official party. From Seaburn, the convoy returned to Wheatsheaf Depot, with No 86 being the last car to arrive. All the

The last night of Sunderland's trams: No 86, suitably decorated, makes its final journey.
Tony Wickens/Online Transport Archive (1565)

surviving cars were scrapped, with the exception of No 100 that was secured for preservation.

Sunderland Depots

Sunderland possessed two tramway depots after the Second World War, one north and the other south of the River Wear crossing. The northern one, Wheatsheaf, was also the location of the corporation's main workshops; this facility survived as a tramway running shed and works until the system's final closure on 1 October 1954. The second depot, Hylton Road, was situated on the circular route via Millfield. In 1943 the building suffered damage as a result of German action during the war. The depot lost its tramcar allocation on 3 January 1954 when the Circle route was converted to bus operation.

Sunderland Closures

5 November 1950
Villette Road

2 September 1951
Southwick

30 November 1952
Grangetown

3 January 1954
Circle; Seaburn (via Roker)

28 March 1954
Durham Road

1 October 1954
Seaburn (via Fulwell)

Sunderland Fleet

2-9

Originally built as Ilford Corporation Nos 33-40 in 1932, these eight trams

In 1938 Sunderland acquired eight cars second-hand from the LPTB. These cars, Nos 2-9, had been delivered six years earlier to Ilford Corporation and were rendered surplus in London as a result of the LPTB's tram to trolleybus conversion programme. No 4 is pictured here at the Durham Road terminus; although all eight survived into 1954, No 4 did not survive until the system's final closure. R. W. A. Jones/Online Transport Archive (SN18)

passed to the London Passenger Transport Board in 1933 (Nos 33-40) before being sold to Sunderland in 1938 following the trial of ex-Ilford No 38 (Sunderland No 7) to the north-east in 1937. The eight cars were fitted with Brush bodies on Peckham P22 trucks. In accordance with usual practice in London at the time, the cars had closed balconies but open lower-deck vestibules. The cars were fitted with modified staircases and vestibules in Sunderland, and also received replacement M&T Hornless trucks between 1946 and 1949. All eight survived until 1954 with Nos 2 and 5 surviving until the final closure.

13-18

These six were originally delivered as open-top cars with ER&TCW bodies

on Brill 22E bogies. The bogies were replaced by Brill 21E four-wheel trucks in 1901. The cars were rebuilt as fully enclosed between 1920 and 1922 when they received Brill Radiax trucks. Further work between 1930 and 1934 saw the trucks again changed, this time to M&T Swing-link (No 13), Peckham P22 (Nos 14/15/18), Peckham P35 (No 16; later converted to P22) and English Electric Swing-link (No 17). All were withdrawn in 1953 with the exception of No 13, which succumbed in January 1954. Although not preserved at the time, the

No 17, seen here passing under the railway bridge on the Circle route, was one of a batch of six cars delivered originally in 1901 and fully enclosed in the early 1920s. By the date of the photograph No 17 was operating on an English Electric Swing-link four-wheel truck. The Circle route was converted to bus operation on 3 January 1954, but No 17 was withdrawn the previous year. R. W. A. Jones/Online Transport Archive (SN54)

body of No 16 was subsequently rescued and restored for use at Beamish.

19-20

Originally Accrington Corporation Nos 42/43 of 1926, these two fully enclosed

In 1931 Sunderland acquired two fully enclosed trams from Accrington Corporation. Before entry into service, these cars were regauged from 4ft 0in to standard gauge. One of the two, No 19, is seen here at Southwick. R. W. A. Jones/Online Transport Archive (SN38)

One of the two cars built in 1933 from the bodyshells of trams acquired from Mansfield, No 21, is seen alongside one of the ex-Ilford Corporation cars, No 6, at the junction of Soothill Terrace and Western Hill. The two trams are operating on the Durham Road route with No 21 heading southbound towards the terminus. The tracks curving to the west were those that carried the Circle route. No 21 survived in service until 1953. R. W. A. Jones/Online Transport Archive (SN43)

trams were acquired in 1931. Fitted with Brush bodies on Peckham RB trucks, the two cars had to be regauged from Accrington's 4ft 0in to standard gauge before entering service. Both cars were withdrawn in the first half of 1953.

21/24

Although built in Sunderland's own workshops at Hylton Road in 1933, these two cars incorporated the English Electric-built bodyshells of two cars acquired from Mansfield (Nos 27/28) that had been new in 1925. Nos 21/24 were fitted with EMB lightweight trucks, and survived in service until 1953 (No 21) and October 1954 (No 24).

22/23/25

These three cars were the survivors of a batch (Nos 19-26) that were delivered in 1901 as four-wheel single-deckers with bodies supplied by ER&TCW on Brill 21E trucks. No 22 was used as a welding car between 1914 and 1925 when it, along with Nos 23 and 25, were converted into fully enclosed double-deckers at Hylton Road with P22 trucks. The remaining single-deck cars were withdrawn in 1930 or 1933 (No 24 had been used as the welding car post-1925).

The last new trams acquired by Huddersfield Corporation were eight fully enclosed English Electric cars delivered during 1931 and 1932. Destined for a relatively short life in Yorkshire, the eight were sold to Sunderland in 1938. Seven, including No 33 see here at the Seaburn (via Roker) terminus, survived until the system's final closure. The car is seen in the red and cream livery adopted in 1937; before that date Sunderland trams were maroon and cream. Phil Tatt/Online Transport Archive (PTP23)

No 22 was one of three survivors of a batch of eight cars delivered in 1901. Originally built as a single-decker, No 22 was used as a welding car between 1914 and 1925 after which it was rebuilt as a fully enclosed double-deck car. Its original truck was replaced by a P22 truck in 1931, and is pictured at Hylton Road on 19 April 1947. John Meredith/Online Transport Archive (7/2)

No 22 received an EMB truck in 1931 and No 25 was fitted with an M&T Swing-link truck two years later; No 22 was re-equipped with an M&T truck in 1936. Withdrawal for Nos 22/23/25 came in early 1954.

26-28

These three fully enclosed trams were delivered in 1935. They were built with bodies constructed at Hylton Road on EMB Hornless trucks and were the first

Sunderland trams to be fitted with glass roof-lights. All three were withdrawn during the first half of 1953 as they were due for overhaul.

29-36

Acquired from Huddersfield Corporation in 1938, these eight fully enclosed trams were the last new cars acquired by Huddersfield, as Nos 137-44, in 1931. They were constructed with English Electric bodies on M&T Swing-link trucks. Before entering service in Sunderland the trams were regauged from Huddersfield's 4ft 7¾in to standard gauge. The first of

the type, No 29, was withdrawn in 1953, but the remaining seven cars survived until the closure of the system with four appearing in the final procession.

No 27 was one of a trio of fully enclosed trams delivered in 1935. It is seen here heading south along Bridge Street while operating a service to Durham Road. The junction here was with the Circle route, with Hylton Road depot situated half a mile to the west. In the background is the Grand Hotel; this imposing Victorian building was closed in 1969 and demolished in 1974. R. W. A. Jones/Online Transport Archive (SN50)

37-42

Sunderland was one of four operators to acquire 'Pilcher' cars following the rundown of the Manchester system. Six of the type were acquired; Nos 37-42 were Manchester Nos 228, 503, 163/76, 380 and 131 respectively. Originally delivered between 1930 and 1932, the six were fitted with Manchester-built bodies on Peckham P35 trucks. The first of the six, No 37, entered service on 22 March 1947. Before entering service all six saw their trolleypoles replaced by pantographs. Two of the type were withdrawn during the first half of 1953

Following their withdrawal in Manchester, the 'Pilcher' cars were sold to four other UK tramway operators; six travelled to north-east England in 1947, becoming Sunderland Corporation Nos 37-42. The last of these cars, No 42 (ex-Manchester No 131), is recorded here at Southwick.
R. W. A. Jones/Online Transport Archive (SN36)

with the remaining four succumbing in January 1954.

43/44

These two cars were the last survivors of a batch of twenty-four cars, Nos 27-50, supplied in 1901. Fitted with open-top bodies supplied by ER&TCW on Brill 21E four-wheel trucks, all were rebuilt with balcony tops between 1904 and 1916. No 32, which was renumbered 43 in 1938, was rebuilt as fully enclosed in 1926, at which time it also received a

replacement P22 truck. No 44 was rebuilt as fully enclosed in 1930 when it also received an EMB Hornless truck. No 44 was withdrawn in 1953 and No 43, which had become a works car in 1951, survived until the system's final closure. A third example of the type, No 46, survived as works car No B until withdrawal in 1951, having been renumbered during the 1930s.

45

Acquired second-hand from Portsmouth Corporation in 1936 and originally numbered 52 (it was renumbered 45 in 1940), this car had a body built in Portsmouth's own workshops on a truck of Portsmouth's own design. Constructed

Sunderland No 43, seen here at Roker on 19 April 1947, was one of two survivors of a batch of cars that had originally been delivered in 1901. No 43 was rebuilt as a fully enclosed car in 1926. Converted to serve as a works car in 1951, No 43 survived until the system's closure in 1954.
John Meredith/Online Transport Archive (8/6)

Sunderland works car No B recorded at Hylton Road Depot on 19 April 1947. This was one of the Dick Kerr-built cars that dated originally to 1901, which had been fitted with a balcony top before the First World War and converted to a works car before the Second World War.
John Meredith/Online Transport Archive (8/1)

Designed as a prototype for fleet modernisation in Portsmouth, No 45 was acquired following the conversion of the South Coast system to trolleybus operation in 1936. Built originally in 1930, the tram was regauged from 4ft 7¾in to standard gauge before operation in Sunderland. The car is seen here on the Fulwell route.
R. W. A. Jones/Online Transport Archive (SN15)

The most modern tramcar in the South Shields fleet made the short journey from Tyneside to Wearside in 1946 when it became Sunderland No 48. It is seen here at Southwick. R. W. A. Jones/Online Transport Archive (SN44)

as a prototype for fleet modernisation, Portsmouth No 1 was destined to be unique as the operator decided to abandon trams in favour of trolleybuses. The car received a replacement EMB truck in 1938. As No 45, the car survived until withdrawal in early 1953.

48

This Brush-bodied centre-entrance streamlined tram was acquired second-hand from South Shields; it reached Wearside on 21 May 1946. It remained in service in Sunderland until January 1954 when it was withdrawn for scrap.

49-52

This quartet of streamlined centre-entrance trams dated to 1938 (Nos 49-51) and 1940 (No 52). Although the bodies were of English Electric design, they were built at Hylton Road on English Electric FL32 trucks. These were the last new trams acquired by Sunderland and were withdrawn in June 1953 (Nos 50/51) and January 1954 (Nos 49 and 52).

53-55

These three streamlined centre-entrance cars entered service in 1935 and 1936. Nos 54 and 55 were both fitted with M&T trucks, but with bodies built by Sunderland Corporation and Brush

No 50 was one of four centre-entrance bogie trams constructed by Sunderland Corporation using frames and bogies supplied by English Electric in 1938 and 1940. The last wholly new trams built for the system, none survived until the end as Sunderland elected to operate its final route using older, non-streamlined cars.
J. Joyce/Online Transport Archive (JT75)

Sunderland breakdown car No C, formerly passenger car No 65, is seen at Hylton Road Depot on 19 April 1947. John Meredith/Online Transport Archive (7/6)

One of three centre-entrance trams to enter service in 1935 and 1936, No 54 was fitted with a corporation-built body fitted onto Maley & Taunton trucks. It is seen here alongside No 23, one of three double-deck cars that had been rebuilt from four-wheel single-deckers, on Kyall Road, part of the Circle route. There had been plans, never completed, for a northern extension off Kyall Road to the North Eastern Railway station at Pallion. This station closed in 1964 but a new station, located close to it, now serves the Tyne & Wear Metro. R. W. A. Jones/Online Transport Archive (SN55)

respectively, and No 53 had an English Electric body on an English Electric truck. No 54 was withdrawn in early 1954, and Nos 53/55 survived until January 1954.

56/57, 60-64, C and D

These nine cars were the survivors of a batch of ten supplied as open-top, but enclosed-vestibule, four-wheelers in 1902. Bodywork was supplied by ER&TCW on Brill 21E trucks. Nos 56-60 and 65 were rebuilt as fully enclosed on P22 trucks between 1926 and 1929. Nos 62-64 were rebuilt as fully enclosed during 1933 and 1934; No 62 received a P22 truck at the same time, and Nos 63 and 64 received English Electric FL32 trucks. No 61 was rebuilt in 1934 with a short top cover and P22 truck; it was nicknamed the 'Turret' thereafter. No 58 became a works car

in 1930 and was withdrawn eight years later. Nos 59 and 65, were transferred to works duties as C and D, before the Second World War. No 62 along with C and D were withdrawn in 1951; five of the remaining cars were withdrawn during 1953, leaving the last of the type, No 63, to be withdrawn in early 1954.

66-71

This batch of six trams was originally delivered in 1906 with open-balcony but enclosed-vestibule, bodies supplied by Brush on M&G radial four-wheel trucks. All were rebuilt during 1923 and 1924 as fully enclosed, and were again modified between 1932 and 1934. At this

In 1906 a batch of six cars, Nos 66-71, were delivered from Brush. All were fully enclosed between 1923 and 1924 and, a decade later, were further modified with replacement trucks. No 71, seen here, was fitted with an EMB Hornless four-wheel truck at that time and used to test equipment used later on Nos 87-98. R. W. A. Jones/Online Transport Archive (SN58)

trucks, and No 68 received an English Electric FL32 and No 71 an EMB Hornless. No 70 was subsequently fitted with an English Electric FL32 truck. No 71 was the testbed of equipment planned for a batch of 12 new trams, Nos 87-98, that had been ordered. Five of the six trams were withdrawn during the first half of 1953

stage the cars were fitted with replacement trucks; Nos 66, 67, 69 and 70 received P22

In 1921 a batch of twelve fully enclosed cars, Nos 72-83, was delivered to Sunderland by English Electric. Most were eventually fitted with EMB Swing-link four-wheel trucks, although No 79, illustrated here en route to Grangetown, was briefly fitted with a P35.
R. W. A. Jones/Online Transport Archive (SN45)

**Sunderland No
84** was a single car
constructed in the
workshops at Hylton
Road in 1926. Its
body incorporated the
lower deck of a tram
originally supplied to
Sunderland District
Electric Tramways.
No 84 is seen among
the crowds at Seaburn
with a service for
Fawcett Street.
Phil Tatt/Online Transport
Archive (673)

with the sole survivor, No 71, succumbing
in January 1954.

72-83

Supplied with fully enclosed English
Electric bodies on Peckham P22 trucks,
this batch of twelve 'forward entrance'
cars entered service in 1921. All were
rebuilt between 1929 and 1931 with
modified vestibules and staircases. All
were retrucked at the same time as they
were rebuilt, receiving EMB swing-axle
trucks with the exception of Nos 77 and

The original No 85
was an experimental
single-deck car that was
built in 1931 for use
on the Villette Road
route. Originally built
with a conventional
trolley pole, the car is
shown here following
modification to use a
bow collector. Stored
at the start of the
Second World War, No
85 was sold to Leeds
in November 1944 and
ultimately became the
basis of the third Leeds
single-deck car, No 600.
Barry Cross Collection/Online
Transport Archive

The last tram to enter service in Sunderland was, appropriately, a final second-hand car, this time from Bury. No 85 entered service in Sunderland in 1948 and survived until 1954, being the last car to operate over the Circle route in January 1954. R. W. A. Jones/Online Transport Archive (SN22)

81 that received Peckham P35s. No 79 also operated with a P35 truck for about two years. Eight of the type were withdrawn during the first half of 1953, with three succumbing in January 1954. The last survivor, No 80, was withdrawn at final closure in October 1954.

84

This single car was built in Hylton Road during 1926 and its fully enclosed body incorporated the lower deck from a 1908-built car that had been supplied to

Pictured at Seaburn, No 86 was nicknamed the 'Ghost Tram' and ultimately became Sunderland's official last tram when the system was finally abandoned in October 1954. R. W. A. Jones/Online Transport Archive (SN10)

Sunderland District Electric Tramways. It was fitted with a Peckham P22 truck originally, but this was replaced by an EMB Flexible axle truck in 1931. No 84 survived until early 1953.

85 (i)

Built with a Brush single-deck body as an experimental car in 1931 on Brush maximum traction bogies, No 85 was

The twelve cars delivered during 1933, Nos 87-98, were the last traditionally styled four-wheel cars that Sunderland acquired new. Future deliveries were either second-hand or streamlined. However, the batch survived longer than the newer vehicles and all remained in service in 1954. No 91 was one of nine fitted with an English Electric body. The remaining three had bodies built in the corporation's own workshops.
Phil Tatt/Online Transport Archive (PTP10)

designed for use on the Villette Road route. Originally fitted with a trolley pole, this was later replaced by a bow collector. The car was stored with the start of the Second World War and never saw service in Sunderland again; it was sold to Leeds (as No 288) in November 1944.

85 (ii)

The last tram to enter service in Sunderland was a further second-hand acquisition, this time from Bury.

Originally No 30 in the Bury fleet, No 85 was new in 1905 and was sold to Wearside in 1948. The car was an open-balcony car when new, but was rebuilt as fully enclosed in Bury in 1925/26; its original Mountain & Gibson 21E four-wheel truck was replaced by an EMB Swing-link truck in 1930. It was the only air-braked tram to be operated by Bury, a factor that may have attracted Sunderland to its purchase following withdrawal in Lancashire in 1947. The car survived until 1954 and was the last car to operate over

Delivered in 1934, No 99 was built by English Electric. Restored to service in 1946, it reappeared in the pre-war livery of cream and maroon – as opposed to the post-war livery of red and cream – and is seen in this outdated livery at Wheatsheaf on 19 April 1947. John Meredith/Online Transport Archive (7/11)

the Circle route when the service ceased in January of that year.

86

Built in Hylton Works on an EMB Hornless truck, this four-wheel fully-enclosed tram was nicknamed the 'Ghost Tram' as a result both of the secrecy at the time of its construction and because it was very quiet in operation. Regarded as one of the fleet's most prestigious cars, No 86 survived to become the system's official last car in October 1954.

87-98

Based on No 86, this batch of twelve cars was delivered in 1933 with English Electric (Nos 89-95) and Sunderland Corporation (Nos 96-98) bodies on EMB Hornless trucks. All were withdrawn during 1954.

99

Built by English Electric using English Electric equal-wheel bogies, No 99 was a centre-entrance streamlined car that entered service in 1934. Stored during the Second World War, it was repainted in 1946 in the pre-war livery of cream and maroon (as now worn by the preserved No 16 at Beamish). By this date this livery was outdated. No 99 was withdrawn in 1951. Offered for sale, there were no

Sunderland acquired the unique ex-Metropolitan Electric Tramways No 331 – the prototype 'Feltham' – from London Transport in 1937, numbering it 100 on Wearside. Following withdrawal in 1951, the car was preserved and is now part of the National Tramway Museum collection at Crich. J. Joyce/Online Transport Archive (JT76)

takers and it was sold for scrap in early 1953.

100

A single car, No 100 was built by Union Construction Co (UCC) for Metropolitan Electric Tramways (MET) in London in 1931, and was the prototype of the 'Feltham' class built for MET and London United Tramways. Numbered 331 by MET and 2168 by the London Passenger Transport Board, the centre-entrance tram was acquired by Sunderland in 1937. It was fitted with a body and bogies all built by UCC. Again, non-standard and heavy on power, it was mostly used only at times of peak demand. The car was stored during the Second World War and was finally withdrawn from service in 1951. Acquired for preservation in 1952, it is now part of the National Tramway Museum collection restored as MET No 331.

TYNE & WEAR METRO

Although the last conventional trams operated in the north-east of England in 1954, there was a network of electrified suburban railway lines in and around Newcastle. By the late 1960s, however, these third-rail routes suffered from lack of investment and increasingly aged rolling stock. Following local government reorganisation, which had resulted in the creation of the Tyne & Wear Passenger Transport Authority, consideration was given to the replacement of the existing lines with a new rapid transit system. Alongside the conversion of 26 miles of existing railway the plans envisaged the construction of eight miles of new line, including an underground section through central Newcastle as well as a new crossing of the River Tyne.

Work started on construction in 1974 and the first section of the route, from Tynemouth to Haymarket via Whitley Bay, opened on 11 August 1980. This was followed on 10 May 1981 by the section from South Gosforth to Bankfoot. Further extensions were opened on 15 November 1981 (Haymarket to Heworth), 14 November 1982 (St James to Tynemouth via North Shields) and 24 March 1984 (Heworth to South Shields). The network was further extended on 17 November 1991 with the opening of the extension from Bankfoot

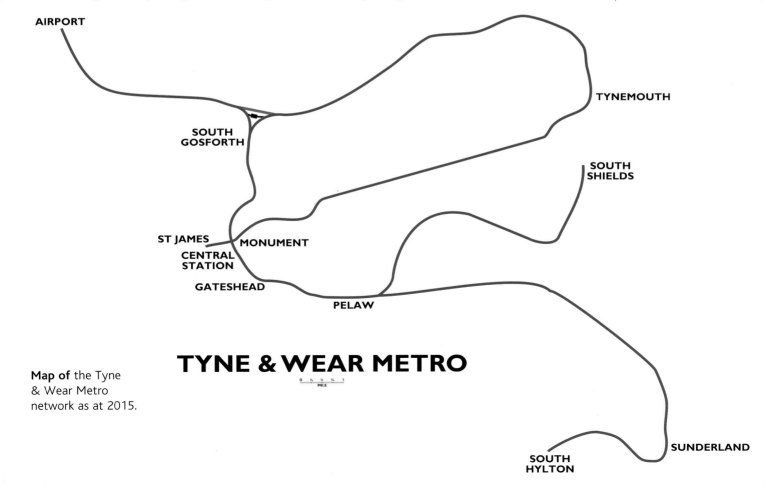

TYNE & WEAR METRO

0 ¼ ½ ¾ 1
MILE

Map of the Tyne & Wear Metro network as at 2015.

Tyne & Wear
Metro No 4053 is pictured in the fleet's original livery on 14 September 1983.
W. C. Janssen/Online Transport Archive

to serve Newcastle Airport, and on 31 March 2002 with the opening of the line from Pelaw to South Hylton via Sunderland. As it stands, the system currently operates over a network of 46 miles in length with 60 stations and a fleet of 90 cars, with the latter all based at one depot located at South Gosforth. Since 2010 the system has been operated by a subsidiary of DB, the German state railways.

Tyne & Wear Depot

The entire fleet is based at South Gosforth, where the system inherited the former British Rail depot used to house the EMUs and DMUs that operated the suburban services before the introduction of the Metro network.

Tyne & Wear Metro Fleet

4001-90

Built by Metro-Cammell at Washwood Heath in Birmingham, the ninety cars

that operate the Tyne & Wear were based on two prototype units, Nos 4001/02, that were built in 1975 and tested on the Metro's test-track before the system opening. The remaining 88 units were delivered between 1978 and 1981. All ninety are single-deck articulated units with the two carriages carried by three bogies. The fleet originally carried a white and yellow livery, into which No 4001 has been restored, but, from the mid-1990s, the cars have carried solid red, green or blue liveries (with, more recently, the doors highlighted in yellow). In 2010 a five-year programme to refurbish the trams started. Originally it was intended that all ninety cars would be treated but this has now been reduced to 86 with four sets left unmodernised. These four, including the two prototype cars, will be retained for emergency use. Following refurbishment, it is expected that the sets will remain in service until the late 2020s.

PRESERVATION

As might be expected, given their relatively late closure, both Leeds and Sheffield are well represented in terms of preserved trams (although in the case of Leeds a number of additional cars that survived the immediate closure in 1959 were unfortunately scrapped in the 1960s). The other tramways featured in this volume are, however, less well represented.

Although no Bradford tram was preserved on closure, No 104 was sold for use at the local rugby league stadium, Odsal, and was secured for preservation in 1953. Using a truck, and other equipment from Sheffield, the tram was restored in Thornbury Works and, when it emerged fully restored in 1958, No 104 represented the first tram in Britain to be restored to an operational condition. For a number of years thereafter No 104 ran regularly on track at Thornbury Works drawing power from the trolleybus overhead. No 104 is now on static display in the city's industrial museum at Moorside Mills in the company of a replica horse car.

Following closure, a number of Gateshead cars were sold for further service on the Grimsby & Immingham

After less than a decade as a scoreboard at Odsal, the body of Bradford No 104 was rescued and restored at Thornbury Works; for a period thereafter, as here on 31 October 1959, the tram was driven up and down track within the works yard. This ceased, however, in the early 1960s, but the tram remained based in Thornbury until after Bradford City Transport disappeared into West Yorkshire PTE, when it was transferred to the city's industrial museum at Moorside Mills, where it remains on static display alongside one of the city's fleet of trolleybuses. John Meredith/ Online Transport Archive (431/7)

Two generations of Leeds four-wheel trams pictured at the National Tramway Museum. In the foreground is 'Beeston Air Brake' No 399; this was built at Kirkstall Road Works in 1925 and was used for a number of years as the works' shunter following withdrawal. Preserved in a relatively poor condition, No 399 was restored to original condition and re-entered service at Crich in 1990. Behind is 'Horsfield' No 180; this car is the only survivor of the 100 cars built during 1931 and 1932.
Vintage Carriages Trust/Online Transport Archive (VCT 7141)

Light Railway. When this line closed in 1961, two of these cars were secured for preservation: No 5 is now based at the National Tramway Museum and No 10 at Beamish. Once part of the National Tramway Museum collection is No 52, a single-deck car that dated originally from 1901; it is now at Beamish. A further body, that of No 51, is extant, although a very long-term restoration project. One of the ex-Sheffield double-deck cars, No 33, was sold for further use after withdrawal. The lower deck was salvaged for preservation and is now at the National

Tramway Museum as Sheffield No 74.

Although no Hull trams were preserved when taken out of service in the East Riding, two of the cars sold to Leeds were secured for preservation. No 132, one of the batch of eleven open-balcony cars built in 1910 that were subsequently rebuilt as fully enclosed, became part of the National Tramway Museum collection. It is at the time of writing on loan to Hull and is on display in the city's Streetlife Museum. A second car, No 96, which had been converted to a single-deck works car and snowplough in 1933, and sold to Leeds in 1945, is now based at the Heaton Park tramway in Manchester.

A number of Leeds trams are preserved, although not all are restored in Leeds livery. Apart from the two ex-Hull cars detailed earlier, a number of trams that operated in Leeds as second-hand from

London Transport have also survived. These include LCC No 1 (ex-Leeds 301) at the National Tramway Museum, and 'Feltham' No 2099 (ex-Leeds No 501) is now part of the London Transport Museum collection. A second ex-Leeds 'Feltham', No 526, is stored at the Seashore Museum, at Kennebunkport in the USA. In terms of trams built for Leeds, there are a number of passenger cars at the National Tramway Museum: horse car No 107 of 1898, 'Hamilton' No 345, 'Beeston Air Brake' No 399, 'Horsfield' No 180 and two of the three single-deck cars, Nos 600 and 602. The National Tramway Museum also houses works car No 2. A number of further Leeds trams were preserved at closure: 'Horsfield' Nos 160 and 202, 'Feltham' No 554 and single-deck No 601 were all saved, but heavy vandalism when stored on the Middleton Railway led to their scrapping in the 1960s.

There are two surviving Newcastle trams. No 102 was secured when the system closed and, after a somewhat peripatetic career (including a period on display at the National Motor Museum at Beaulieu), was moved to Crich in the early 1960s and now forms part of the National Tramway Museum collection. More recently, the body of No 114 was rescued; this has now been fully restored to operational condition and can be seen at Beamish.

The National Tramway Museum has a number of ex-Sheffield trams on display, including No 74 mentioned earlier. Horse car No 15, which dates from 1874, was the first tram to operate at the museum (in 1963). In terms of passenger cars, the collection houses single-deck car No 46 (one of the passenger trams converted to a snowplough now restored to original condition), 'Standard' No 189, 'Domed Roof' No 264 and one of the two 'Roberts' cars, No 510, which was decorated for the closure in October 1960. The museum also houses No 330, a works car that was bought second-hand

from Bradford during the Second World War as a double-deck passenger car and subsequently cut down to single-deck for works use. There are two Sheffield trams based at Beamish: No 264, a 'Preston' car dating from 1907, and the second surviving 'Roberts' car, No 513. The latter, now shorn of its commemorative artworks marking the system's closure, operated at Blackpool for some years and is now on indefinite loan to the East Anglian Transport Museum near Lowestoft. The final Sheffield survivor is the body of No 460, which was one of the batch of cars supplied by Cravens in 1926/27. It was sold following withdrawal, and the lower deck was salvaged by the South Yorkshire Transport Museum in 1987.

When the Sunderland system was abandoned in 1954 only one tram was secured for preservation – No 100, the prototype London 'Feltham' car No 331. This tram, now restored to its London condition, is on display at the National Tramway Museum. A second Sunderland tram – No 16, one of the batch delivered in 1900 – was subsequently rescued and restored at the North of England Museum at Beamish, where it now operates over the museum's tramway in the purple and cream livery used by the corporation before 1937.

It is still possible to travel on a Gateshead, Sunderland or Newcastle tram in the north-east of England courtesy of the museum at Beamish. Examples from all three fleets operate regularly at the museum. Here Gateshead No 10, one of the single-deck cars that was preserved after operation on the Grimsby & Immingham line, loads passengers in the museum's townscape on 19 September 2003. Author (8515)

BIBLIOGRAPHY

A Nostalgic look at Leeds Trams since 1950; Graham H. E. Twidale; Silver Link; 1991

A Nostalgic look at North-East Trams since the 1940s; Christopher R. Irwin; Silver Link; 1990

A Nostalgic look at Sheffield Trams since 1950; Graham H. E. Twidale; Silver Link; 1995

Bradford City Tramways; D. M. Coates; Wyvern Publications; 1984

Bradford Corporation Tramways; J. S. King; Venture Publications; 1998

British & Irish Tramway Systems since 1945; Michael H. Waller and Peter Waller; Ian Allan Publishing; 1992

Huddersfield Corporation Tramways; Roy Brook; published by the author; 1983

Keighley Corporation Transport; J. S. King; Advertiser Press Ltd; 1964

Leeds Transport: Volume 2 – 1902-1931; J. Soper; Leeds Transport Historical Society; 1996

Leeds: A History of its Tramways; Noel Proudlock; published by the author; 1991

Modern Tramway; Light Railway Transport League; 1945 onwards

One Hundred Years of Leeds Tramways; Andrew D. Young; Turntable Enterprises; 1970

Sheffield Corporation Tramways; Kenneth Gandy; Sheffield City Libraries; 1985

The Classic Trams; Peter Waller; Ian Allan Ltd; 1993

The Directory of British Tram Depots; Keith Turner, Shirley Smith and Paul Smith; OPC; 2001

The Golden Age of Tramways; Charles F. Klapper; Routledge & Kegan Paul; 1961

The Tramways of Gateshead; George S. Hearse; published by the author; 1965

The Tramways of Gateshead; George S. Hearse; published by the author; 1965

The Tramways of Jarrow and South Shields; George S. Hearse; published by the author; 1971

The Tramways of Northumberland; George S. Hearse; published by the author; 1960

The Tramways of Sunderland; S. A. Staddon; Advertiser Press, Huddersfield; 1964

The Tramways of West Yorkshire; J. C. Gillham and R. J. S. Wiseman; Light Rail Transit Association; undated

The Trolleybuses of Newcastle upon Tyne 1935-1966; T. P. Canneaux and N. H. Hanson; Newcastle upon Tyne City Libraries; 2nd ed; 1985

Tram to Supertram; Peter Fox, Paul Jackson and Roger Benton; Platform 5; 1995

Trams around Dewsbury & Wakefield; Norman Ellis; Wharncliffe Books; 2004

Tramway Review; Light Railway Transport League; 1950 onwards